GW01374640

THE NO-FAIL
MISSION

The University of Toledo Press
www.utoledopress.com

Copyright 2024
By The University of Toledo Press
All rights reserved

Manufactured in the United States of America

THE NO-FAIL MISSION
The Men and Women Behind the Presidential Service Badge

By Anthony Knopps

The Presidential Service Badge Foundation is focused on preserving the memories of these silent sentinels of our freedom and the "No-Fail Missions" that they led. The author's royalties are earmarked for a scholarship fund for children of Presidential Service Badge recipients. To learn more or to make a donation yourself, visit thenofailmission.com

No part of this book may be reproduced or transmitted in any form or by any means, electronic or mechanical, including photocopying, recording, or by any information storage and retrieval system without permission in writing from the publisher.

Edited by Yarko Kuk
Project assistance by Gracie Brown, Erin Czerniak, and Kennedy Lovell
Book design by Stephanie Delo

Hardcover ISBN: 979-8-8229-5116-7
Paperback ISBN: 979-8-8229-5117-4
eBook ISBN: 979-8-8229-5118-1

THE NO-FAIL MISSION

The Men and Women Behind the Presidential Service Badge

ANTHONY KNOPPS

To Former Secretary of State and Presidential Service Badge
holder Colin Powell who taught all of us that
"there are no secrets to success.
It (success) is the result of preparation,
hard work and learning from failure."

TABLE OF CONTENTS

Prologue ix

CHAPTER 1: #Boston Strong 1
   Erica P. Cooper, Presidential Service Badge #27327

CHAPTER 2: America is Under Attack 17
   Ivan Lagares-Gomez, Presidential Service Badge #17801

CHAPTER 3: Eighteen Acres 29
   Rob Cole, Presidential Service Badge #19620

CHAPTER 4: My dad told me, "You are not coming home" 37
   Jonée Coleman, Presidential Service Badge #22353

CHAPTER 5: You're a part of history 49
   Jeff Worthington, Presidential Service Badge #27034

CHAPTER 6: I grew up on G.I. Joe 73
   Roy Flores, Presidential Service Badge #27450

CHAPTER 7: Tomorrow can be a Better Day 83
   Hervy "James" Oxendine, Presidential Service Badge #20138

CHAPTER 8: Service is a Family Affair 103
   Scott Jones, Presidential Service Badge #19406

CHAPTER 9: Hail to the Chef 119
   Martin C.J. "Marti" Mongiello, Presidential Service Badge #14592

CHAPTER 10: One team, one fight 133
   Seth Rawson, Presidential Service Badge #19798

Epilogue 155

From the Author 161

PROLOGUE

> *"It's only when you hitch your wagon to something larger than yourself that you realize your true potential."*
>
> –Barack Obama, 44th President of the United States
> May 25, 2008, Middletown, Connecticut
> Wesleyan University Graduation

For the men and women who have earned the Presidential Service Badge (PSB), this notion of something larger than self is more than just a phrase, it's part of their DNA. Established in 1964 by President Lyndon Johnson, the Presidential Service Badge replaced the White House Service Badge established four years earlier by President Dwight Eisenhower.

The PSB is considered one of the highest honors one can achieve in the military. However, it's largely unknown when compared to such recognition as the Purple Heart, Bronze Star, or Navy Cross. The Presidential Service Badge is awarded upon recommendation of the Military Assistant to the President to any member of the Armed Forces who serves at least one year assigned to duty in the White House Office or to military units that support the Office of the President. It is designed to recognize meritorious service "above and beyond" the normal scope of a servicemember's duties.

Just occupying the role for at least one year is not enough to earn the Presidential Service Badge. The work these people do has to have had made a major difference in supporting the Office of the President.

"It's not just about making it through that first year," said PSB recipient Erica Cooper. "What it's saying is that in the first year, you've learned what you need to learn. You've been able to handle that amount of stress. You've learned to handle the pressure. You've learned things about the President that you needed to recognize and understand safely so you could support the President. You needed to understand the history of whatever role you are in and really appreciate it and respect it to a degree that you are essential in some small way.

Those so honored with the Presidential Service Badge are the only ones allowed to wear the Presidential Seal or "Coat of Arms" on their military dress or on their civilian clothes. There are only two exceptions: Uniformed members of the U.S. Secret Service and the President himself. Since its inception nearly 60 years ago, just over 20,000 people have received the PSB. These folks are a cross-section of America, both men and women, different races and faiths. There is not one picture of a "typical recipient."

As a result, the stories of these Presidential Service Badge recipients are as diverse as the people behind the badge itself. They come from cities and towns across the United States, from rich communities and from poor communities, from places big and small. They arrive at the White House with a singular purpose: to achieve their "no-fail" mission each day. The hours are long, the environment stressful, and the outcome uncertain—and they would have it no other way. Many freely admit they were "in the room" when history happened but deflect their role in that history by merely saying they were just "doing their duty." Many of those duties are classified, while others are carried out with little fanfare or attention. They include taking care of the President and his staff when they are on foreign soil. They also include helping to make sure the President has all of the facts currently available to make the best decision for the country and the world.

There have always been questions about exactly what bonds members of a group to one another. We hear of the importance of affection and trust. We hear of the value of the shared experience of overcoming danger. We hear of sharing a mutual goal and of achieving it. In these stories, offered in their own words, you will hear echoes of these concepts as those profiled work to support the Office of the President.

Each of these Presidential Service Badge recipients who have shared their stories here are men and women of strong character and ethical foundations. They are, to a person, humble. They understand the great honor and privilege it is to serve this country, in ways both great and small.

The stories in this book speak to the stress, exhilaration, and yes, even the humor, that comes with being connected to this "beating heart" of American Democracy. Known as the "People's House," those who work on the eighteen acres at 1600 Pennsylvania Avenue and support those who call that address home have a unique history as fascinating as the building itself, if not more so. Each chapter tells the story of a specific PSB recipient's experience, from their point of view, in their own words, as much as possible.

As President George H.W. Bush said at a 2011 ceremony honoring former President Ronald Reagan, "There could be no definition of a successful life that does not include service to others." Enjoy these stories of some of our silent sentinels who served the Office of the President.

CHAPTER 1

#Boston Strong

Erica P. Cooper, Presidential Service Badge #27327

President Barack Obama poses for a photograph with Erica P. Cooper at the White House Oval Office, (Photo courtesy: Erica P. Cooper)

THE NO-FAIL MISSION

Patriots' Day is always a special time in the city of Boston, Massachusetts and so it was again on April 15, 2013. As the clock approached noon, more than 37,000 runners were on course, taking part in the 117th running of the Boston Marathon. The first runners crossed the finish line a little more than an hour later.

The crowds dissipated as the afternoon wore on, but in one of the traditions of the historic race, hundreds of people remained to cheer on each finisher. That spirit of community unifies the people of Boston and of the entire New England area. This race is part of their DNA, their reason for being.

At 2:49 p.m., the clear calm day was shattered by a pair of bombs that were detonated near the finish line. The first detonated in front of the Marathon Sports store at 671 Boylston Street. Thirteen seconds later, the second bomb detonated in front of the Forum Restaurant at 755 Boylston Street, about 180 yards down the course.

When the dust had settled, three people had lost their lives: 23-year-old Lu Lingzi, 29-year-old Krystle Campbell, and eight-year-old Martin Richard. Nearly 300 other people—spectators and runners alike—were injured, some seriously. Within a half hour, all the remaining runners had been cleared from the course.

It didn't take long for the news to begin filtering into the White House, 400 miles away. President Barack Obama received an initial briefing from his Homeland Security team. They also kept him up to date about the events on the ground. As the investigation continued and the search for suspects intensified, the White House was marshalling all its available resources to help find those responsible. The next day, the President updated the American people, and for the first time, he called it an act of terrorism.

That same day, the decision was made to have President Obama visit Boston and to participate in an interfaith service. White House

Spokesman Jay Carney described it as a service "dedicated to those who were gravely wounded or killed in Monday's bombing."

The tragic events of that week hit home for Presidential Service Badge Recipient #27327, Master Sergeant Erica P. Cooper. A veteran of the White House Communications Agency (WHCA), Cooper was one of the event planners for President Obama. Her job was to ensure the Office of the President and Senior White House staff were provided all secure communications required to function successfully, especially in crisis situations.

This trip was more than just a quick visit to a grieving city. For Cooper, it was personal. That grieving city was home. One doesn't always get to choose which Presidential trip to support, but she was offered the opportunity to do so in this case.

"It was a devastating, gut wrenching, and humbling experience, but one that I wanted to be a part of. That day, more than 37,000 runners… family participated in this awesome tradition and within minutes their lives, our lives were shattered forever."

The Boston Marathon is traditionally held on Patriots' Day—the third Monday of April—in recognition of the American Revolutionary War Battles of Lexington and Concord on April 19, 1775. The day is a public holiday in Massachusetts, and it draws hundreds of thousands of people to Boston each year.

Prior to the bombings, Cooper hadn't supported what is known at the White House as "down and dirty" event. A "down and dirty" event happens when a natural disaster or catastrophic event occurs, and the President decides he or she must go to the affected area. During this time, the event is coordinated quickly and in significantly less time making it incredibly stressful. There is really no rest, no stopping, just the pushing through to make it happen. For this "down and dirty", there was an added layer of stress because it was her home.

"More than ever, I wanted to support my people and ensure the President had everything he needed to guarantee it being a 'no fail' event. We needed our President more now than ever and I knew he would provide comfort and touch everyone in a way that only he could. Maybe even take some of our pain away.

"When planning for these events, we know the end result is the President arriving and handling the situation on behalf of our country. But from where I stood, it was like I went through the motions and worked so hard that I didn't have time to process the situation completely. And when you frequently travel, it's event after event after event. It's almost like having tunnel vision. Get in, set up, provide exceptional support, tear down, get out. And on to the next event. It's not until "game day" at each event, when the President is standing a few feet away, the magnitude of it hit me.

"I realized that in that moment, I couldn't lose my military bearing or sight of this critical moment because that's when things go wrong. Instead, I had to maintain a razor-sharp focus. Though honestly, I wanted to just stare in awe at him, cry and jump up and down like a child in excitement! No matter how many event sites I supported, it never got old. Each one felt like the first time."

Cooper grew up not too far from the scene of the Boston Marathon bombing. Her family can trace its roots back to the Cape Verde Islands, an archipelago in the Atlantic that's between 320 and 460 nautical miles from the African Coast. Her grandparents, in search of a better life for their family, migrated, then eventually settled, in Cape Cod, Massachusetts. Her mother was a first generation American. It was a good fit, for many reasons.

"I grew up around what I feel is a melting pot of people and we all accepted one another. Though I am proud and very grounded in my Portuguese/Cape Verdean roots, I loved meeting and learning about people from other cultures. On the Cape, everyone I met had at least heard of Portuguese and/or Cape Verdean people because there's approximately 70,000 Cape Verdeans in Massachusetts, while others live within the other New England states. It was common to appreciate our food, traditions, and culture throughout the Cape in the form of festivals, food or while supporting events at our Cape Verdean Club.

"When I joined the military my sense of security and self was shaken because I found it difficult to connect with my peers and it was impossible to meet people like me. I was judged in ways I didn't understand. My African American peers would tell me, 'You don't belong with us because you don't act, look like or talk like us.' Whereas Caucasian peers told me, 'You kind of sound like us, but you definitely don't look like us.' When I spoke to people on the phone, and later met them in person they'd always say, 'Oh, I thought you were white!' In my twenty-four years of Air Force service, no matter what country or state I was in, whether I moved there or deployed; the treatment was always the same. I didn't fit in to any group of people and that made it even harder to make friends and find my place in life.

"In addition to not being able to find my place within the different nationalities and ethnicities in the military, I also struggled with finding confidence within myself. I think as a female, person of color and someone who grew up in a single parent home all contributed to my lack of confidence and self-esteem. My mum was an amazing woman who had no choice but to raise six children alone when my father left after I was born. We grew up on welfare and lived in government housing my entire young life. As a child, I dreamed of "more" though I didn't know what that looked like or how to get there."

To find that "more," Cooper often retreated into the literary world. She fell in love with writing and the escape that it provided.

"I always wanted to be an author. I used to write poetry all the time. I had one poem published in the Library of Congress, which I was so proud of. I felt internally that I had so much to say, but I didn't know what platform I could do that from successfully."

That "escape" eventually came in the form of the military and the career it offered. It was a move that surprised even her closest friends.

"As a teenager, I worked at McDonald's. And, after joining the military when I went home on leave, classmates and friends would tell me, 'I swear, I thought you were going to work at McDonald's for the rest of your life!' I was grateful for the opportunity to work at McDonald's, and I learned so many valuable skills that I used while serving, but at home, I was shy, awkward, a nerd and a band geek and no one expected much of me in terms of success as an adult."

To work for the President of the United States, you must apply for the position. Then each person competes against their peers in the same career field and branch of service. It's a lengthy, time-consuming, and difficult process. During the interview phase investigators go back many years to investigate and adjudicate the security clearance needed to support the President. During this phase, Cooper found it unnerving, not only for her, but for many of her family, friends, and acquaintances.

"I remember a teacher from middle school calling my mum and asking her for my phone number. She was worried about me after meeting "a man in a suit" who asked a lot of questions about me. I couldn't tell her what was happening because I was still going through the qualification process. I tried my best to convince her everything was OK, but I don't think she believed me. When I finally got the job, I was able to let her know why they visited. She was so very excited for me."

When Cooper started working at the WHCA (White House Communications Agency), she was finally able to feel like she found her "place."

"At WHCA, I was there because I was handpicked. I applied for the position and competed against my peers in my Branch of Service. I understood that if I was selected that I was entering into something far greater and more honorable than I'd ever experienced. You see, only the top 1 percent of military members for each branch of service receives the honor of serving the Office of the President of the United States. When I learned that I was going to WHCA, I didn't believe it. I didn't tell my mum or anyone else right away because I was convinced someone would come back and say they were just kidding, or they made a mistake! When I got orders (the paperwork needed to move from one location to another) that's when I felt safe enough to tell everyone. When I called my mum and told her that I was going to work for the President, she told everyone! She was so wicked proud!"

"Serving at the WHCA was my best assignment hands down for so many reasons. Something that was so important, and I appreciate to this day, is it was the first time in my adult life that I wasn't judged by my skin color, sex, ethnicity or where I came from. I was thankful that my evaluations were based solely on my job performance and capabilities."

Cooper was selected to be part of the President's journey to Boston, a mission that was both exhilarating, but also stressful.

"At times while supporting this mission, I didn't know if I could mentally and emotionally maneuver through it. I had to remain focused on the task at hand and remind myself that I had to keep moving forward for those who died, were injured, my family related by blood and those willing to stand by me when the world felt like it was ending. Giving up was not negotiable and people like the Massport Operations Team at Logan Airport gave me strength, food, hugs, and inspiration to keep going. One thing I've always been proud of about my home is we have each other's back. Always. When I started preparing for the visit, and reached out to people, as soon as they heard my "Boston accent," they went above and beyond to be there for me. They obviously wanted to support the President, but they did things they didn't have to do to support me. They checked on me, asked me if I'd eaten, if they could help me in any way. They watched over me. Even after the President left and I returned to Washington D.C. that bond that was created was still strong. In fact, to this day, we're all still friends! The support, sense of family, connections I've made at WHCA is like nothing I've ever experienced. I would do anything for those I served with and there's no doubt that we're all family.

"When one is lucky enough to find a place that allows you to become the best version of yourself, it's something that sticks with you."

For Cooper, that was the case with her time at the White House. It was that sense of camaraderie that was instilled in her on her very first day and continued to grow with each event. She supported the President on many trips, both stateside and abroad. The Boston trip was clearly a memorable one, filled with a range of emotions including peace and pride. As she was securing Air Force One, she received a call from someone very close to her, her mum.

"I was walking under the plane behind the tire," Cooper said, recalling the conversation. "And my mum called my cell phone. Of course, when mum calls…you answer! She said, 'where are you?'

"I said, 'I'm in DC.'

"'No, you're not' she answered.

When you support a Presidential trip, you don't share the travel details until the President's schedule is shared with the public. Because this trip was a "down and dirty," Cooper couldn't tell anyone where she was going.

"When I left D.C., the schedule hadn't yet been released, and when I touched down in Boston, I hit the ground running. There was no time to tell anyone. On "game day" when the President was descending the stairs off Air Force One, I was walking under the plane. A local news station briefly captured my back and my mum happened to be watching the news at the same time. She instantly recognized me and called me. I was shocked! Though I didn't get to see or hug her, her voice instantly made me feel comfort, safety and at peace. It was just what I needed to give me the extra strength to get through the event. It felt amazing to hear her tell me how proud she was of me."

Before the President arrives at an event site, there are teams that fly ahead to ensure everything is set up prior to his arrival. There are so many moving pieces. To the outside world it could look quite chaotic but to these experts, everything is meticulously planned to the smallest detail.

"I always tried to accomplish my piece of the puzzle ahead of time as I found it very interesting and exciting to watch all key organizations finalize their roles and the event unfold. The work was hard but fun. I remember when we first arrived at the location, we'd start the initial meetings and set up. At the beginning we wore regular street clothes. People had no idea who we were. We quietly went about our business with little interaction from outsides sources. Offices were transformed, and as the days progressed closer to "game day" our attire changed to professional attire. We might start with a nice shirt and pants, the next day, perhaps a nice shirt, pants, and a sweater, and on game day it was a full suit.

"In the beginning when you had to work with civilian organizations like hotels you'd do as much as you could independently. You'd tell them what you needed and quietly coordinate things. When the time got closer to "game day" and if the President was staying at a specific hotel for example, then, I'd have to meet with the management. At that meeting, it's the first time you acknowledge who you are."

"I'd say something like, 'My name is Erica Cooper and I work for the Office of the President of the United States. The President will be staying at your hotel, so there are some things we need to discuss to ensure this visit is successful.' You remind the staff that the conversation is confidential until told otherwise and get right to business."

"It was always fun to see the look on everyone's faces when they realized what was really going on. My first time having this conversation, I had to hold everything together inside. When I saw their eyes light up, I wasn't prepared for that. I just had a script in my head, and I went through it. And when they were responding in a very excited manner, I had to keep my bearing and maintain professionalism when I wanted to say 'I know, right! Can you believe it?!'"

"For me, it didn't matter how many events I supported. Each one felt like the first time. And that internal excitement never left. I think even the most senior members would say the same thing. It was such an honor and awesome experience!"

"Sometimes while I was working, the President would walk in and when I caught that first glimpse…it was insane! It was scary, exciting, surreal, overwhelming, awesome, and shocking that he was standing right there in front of me! You must keep your military bearing at all times but in those moments, it was so hard! I remember times when he said hello and I'd start shaking. Sometimes, I would stare, and words felt like they wouldn't come out of my mouth for hours. I prayed I didn't look or sound like an absolute fool!"

That excitement also translated to the arriving airport where Cooper was often trusted to let others know just where the President was and when he was landing.

"When Air Force One was arriving, I had the honor of "calling arrival." It was my responsibility to inform everyone at each location that the President landed. Scary to do, but such an honor. It was truly one of the coolest things I've ever gotten to do."

Despite the countless hours and high stress, Cooper tried to keep the trips lighthearted and relaxed, especially with her family. She often played games with her children, long after "Where in the world is Carmen San Diego?" was popular.

"While supporting a Presidential trip, the location cannot be discussed until it's formally released to the public. So, when I had to leave my husband, son, and daughter, I tried to find ways to make them feel like they were part of the 'adventure.' I'd have them guess my location. To start with, I'd create difficult clues so they couldn't find me right away—and they couldn't use the Internet. As the days progressed, and the location was released, I'd provide easier clues. They always found me, and the end result was a prize from the location when I returned."

The go-go-go lifestyle that Cooper and other Presidential Service Badge recipients endured during their time serving the Office of the President came with its own set of challenges and even tribulations. The divorce rate is high for those who take on roles like this. Even those with the strongest of marriages are torn between their personal and professional lives.

"Sadly, I was one of them," said Cooper. "My ex and I are friends now. But, at the time, I felt horrible for all the times that I had to leave him and my children behind. At times it was difficult managing being a wife, a mum, servicemember, and someone supporting the President of the United States."

That's the challenge in any role, but especially a role like this. Life goes on. Deaths in the family still happen. Marriages, births, graduations, even school concerts still happen. And you can't be there for everything.

"Though I had this amazing position, it didn't stop problems from brewing at home. College assignments were still due—I was working on my master's degree at the time. Other job responsibilities at home still had to be accomplished while traveling. At times, it was hard to juggle all of that. The leadership at the Agency did try, whenever possible, to allow us to go home if an emergency occurred while we were on travel. But sometimes it couldn't happen immediately or at all.

"Life just happens. Some days you wake up feeling great, while others you feel bad. But, in this role, you had to just keep moving forward."

"My kids were young, so I made it a point to always call home. It was difficult on the days that I sacrificed sleep to spend time with them. When they cried because they wanted me to come home, I felt helpless and alone. Many times, I felt like a bad mum, and when they didn't want to talk to me, it crushed my soul. I hated when they were sick because I wasn't there to make it all better. It became the norm to miss events like birthdays, school concerts, field days and tucking them in at night. Still, I did my best to call and wake them every morning and to wish them a good night, even if it was only for a few minutes.

"In a lifestyle like this it's understandable how spouses grow tired of the demands and having to put their personal and professional lives on hold to keep the home running. It's easy to forget that it's not "you" intentionally trying to sabotage them; it's just part of the job. As much as my ex tried, it became too much. I think my position was a bit intimidating as well. When people only talk about what you do and forget the spouse, that becomes an added layer to an already sensitive situation. My ex was just taking off in his career and wanted to accomplish so much more. But my career didn't allow him room to grow professionally."

"I felt like we were always in a professional competition, though I wasn't interested in competing. I also felt guilty as a woman having such an amazing opportunity because people compared his accomplishments as a man with mine, which was totally unfair. As much as I tried to build him up it just wasn't enough."

"I think it's important to point out that I'm grateful that my daughter is a very strong and beautiful human being who isn't afraid to chase her dreams. I know that she can handle anything in life because of the example that I set. And now that she's older, we've been able to have conversations about living in D.C.

"At 23, she has acknowledged that she didn't appreciate the things I did for her at such a young age, and she didn't understand why I always abandoned her.

"To date, she recognizes the sacrifices I made was to give her and her brother the best opportunities in life. I'm proud and thankful that my kids are so well-rounded, strong, amazing, understanding, sweet, kind, brilliant young adults. That makes the sacrifices so worth it."

"Concerning my ex and I, I do feel guilty and bad at times. I also try to give myself grace because we weren't in the best place prior to moving to D.C. and I think the challenges of the assignment at WHCA was the last straw. I'm happy that we're friends and I will always wish him the very best."

Some describe the last day serving the Office of the President as a weight being lifted off their shoulders. Still, they revere the job and its "no-fail" mission by gladly extending their service. Cooper was one of them, agreeing to a two-year extension of her original assignment.

Ironically, without that extension Cooper would not have been a part of the President's trip to Boston during that horrific time. She would not have been able to support the office as President Obama worked to heal a wounded city and nation during the interfaith prayer service of April 18, 2013.

"You've shown us, Boston, that in the face of evil, Americans will lift up what's good," the President said. "In the face of cruelty, we will choose compassion. In the face of those who would visit death upon innocents, we will choose to save and to comfort and to heal. We'll choose friendship. We'll choose love.

"Scripture teaches us, "God has not given us a spirit of fear and timidity, but of power, love, and self-discipline."

"And that's the spirit you've displayed in recent days. When doctors and nurses, police, and firefighters and EMTs and Guardsmen run towards explosions to treat the wounded—that's discipline.

"When exhausted runners, including our troops and veterans—who never expected to see such carnage on the streets back home—become first responders themselves, tending to the injured—that's real power.

"When Bostonians carry victims in their arms, deliver water and blankets, line up to give blood, open their homes to total strangers, give them rides back to reunite with their families—that's love.

"We'll choose love.

"Scripture teaches us, "God has not given us a spirit of fear and timidity, but of power, love, and self-discipline." And that's the spirit you've displayed in recent days.

"Tomorrow, the sun will rise over Boston. Tomorrow, the sun will rise over this country that we love. This special place. This state of grace.

"Scripture tells us to "run with endurance the race that is set before us." As we do, may God hold close those who've been taken from us too soon. May He comfort their families. And may He continue to watch over these United States of America."

Those words are as powerful today for Cooper as they were when the President first uttered them.

"At that specific moment I remember I was literally crying," she said. "You're not supposed to cry in uniform, but I did. I couldn't stop. I felt the President's words and I felt like we all belonged. We were a family, grieving an awful moment in time. As he spoke, the world hung on his every word. His words lifted and inspired us. We weren't there because of race, or color, sex, religion, or ethnicity. We were there to hear our Commander-In-Chief, our leader speak words of inspiration, hope, faith, strength, unity, love, and peace. And, on that day, I felt like he did just that. I could see it in the level of support I received from absolute strangers. From those who provided for, worried about, looked out for, and loved me from the date of arrival and every day forward, that we were and always will be 'Boston Strong.'"

CHAPTER 2

America is Under Attack

*To Ivan Lagares
With best wishes,*

Ivan Lagares-Gomez, Presidential Service Badge #17801

President George W. Bush poses for a photograph with Ivan Lagares-Gomez at the White House Oval Office, (Photo courtesy: Ivan Lagares-Gomez)

THE NO-FAIL MISSION

For those of us who lived through September 11, 2001, we easily grasp it was a day like no other. The deadliest attack on American soil came during a spectacularly clear day in both New York City and in the nation's capital of Washington D.C. There was a touch of fall in the air that crisp morning.

At 8:46 a.m. EST, the day turned to tragedy when American Airlines Flight 11 was flown into the North Tower of the World Trade Center. What was initially thought to be an horrific accident turned even darker when a second plane, United Airlines Flight 175, struck the South Tower of the World Trade Center at 9:02 a.m. Minutes later, at 9:37 a.m., American Airlines Flight 77, crashed into the Pentagon in Washington D.C. It was a short time later when United Airlines Flight 93 crashed in Shanksville, Pennsylvania.

Hundreds of miles away, President George W. Bush was in Sarasota, Florida. The visit was designed to focus attention on his education efforts. White House Chief of Staff Andrew Card walked in as the President was reading "My Pet Goat" to a group of elementary school children. The words he whispered in the President's ear were clear and concise.

"A second plane has hit the second tower. America is under attack."

For seven minutes, the President remained with the school children even as chaos was building throughout the government. For President Bush, who had been in office only a few months, he was grappling with a range of emotions, but also concern about the children who were in the room. He shared those feelings during an interview a few months later with Oprah Winfrey.

"At first, I was angry," the President told Oprah. "How dare they attack us. And then, I looked at the little kids, and, um, the innocence of the children in the classroom. In contrast to the evil of those who would attack America was vivid. It became clear to me at that time, my job was to protect the people."

For the Secret Service, the goal at that moment was to get the President airborne aboard Air Force One. It was the easiest way to ensure that the President would not become a target on the ground. Before he left, President Bush made a brief statement:

> Today, we've had a national tragedy. Two airplanes have crashed into the World Trade Center in an apparent terrorist attack on our country.
>
> I have spoken to the Vice President, to the Governor of New York, to the Director of the FBI, and have ordered that the full resources of the federal government go to help the victims and their families, and—and to conduct a full-scale investigation to hunt down and to find those folks who committed this act.
>
> Terrorism against our nation will not stand. And now if you would join me in a moment of silence. May God bless the victims, their families, and America. Thank you very much.

As the President boarded Air Force One for a journey that took him hopscotching around the country, Army Sergeant First Class Ivan Lagares-Gomez (Presidential Badge Recipient #17801), was thinking back to what only a few hours ago had been a very quiet morning of a nondescript trip.

"That morning, we went on a run," Lagares-Gomez recalled, before shifting to the chaotic moments as the attack happened. "I mean, all hell broke loose. When they told the President that America is under attack, you can just see his face that he was mad as hell. And then he came to the back, and everyone was talking to him. You saw him take out a notebook and he was writing something in there and then he went up to the front and put out that statement."

As the events of 9/11 unfolded, Lagares-Gomez tried to reach his wife who was working at the Commerce Department. Rumors filled the air around Washington. Among those rumors, reports of a car bomb detonating outside the State Department. While that later proved to be unfounded, the tension was palpable. It was only made worse by his inability to reach his wife, his high school sweetheart.

"We couldn't communicate. I tried to reach through to the people who were getting to the White House. They couldn't communicate with her, either. She actually started walking from the Commerce Department to the Pentagon because there were no vehicles moving. She ended up taking a ride with a stranger to the Pentagon.

"Later, I finally got with her, and she was still shaking."

Lagares-Gomez describes his wife fondly, crediting her with her steadfast support as he took on mission after mission for the Army.

"We've been married for 33 years now. I know in high school that she was the one. We were at different high schools, but we were always together. When we got married, we decided to move from Puerto Rico to Chicago. I used to work at the airport, at O'Hare, but I always wanted to be in the Army.

"I mean, there's always a doubt about what, you know, what is next? I mean, I've done so much. My first year, I was involved in the conflict in Panama, with Noriega. It was my first assignment. I was involved with that. I can tell you stuff about what I did in South America, but…"

Lagares-Gomez was stationed at Fort Lewis in Washington state when he got his orders to report to the White House and to serve the Office of the President. It was a surprise.

"I explained to the Sergeant Major that I had just received orders to go to Germany. We were literally about to move. All of our stuff was already on its way there.

"I explained to him that I was already on orders, and they said, it was not a problem. If you want to come to the White House, we can change them because you qualify. I didn't have the 'Yankee White' clearance, but I did have the top-secret clearance."

"Yankee White" is an administrative nickname for a background check for Department of Defense personnel and contractor employees working with the President and Vice-President. The background check is extensive and is done for those with extremely sensitive positions in support of POTUS and VPOTUS. Such a clearance is considered mandatory for such a role.

"I told him, let me talk to my wife and I will call you back. She agreed and I called him back the next day. The move was good for our families because they were in New York and Florida, and we were going to be in-between. I had never been stationed on the East Coast because I had spent almost three quarters of my time in the Army overseas.

"A lot of people who don't know anything about the military don't realize that I literally spent years away from my family. I went to Panama, to Bosnia, and then multiple deployments in Iraq, that's time away from your family that will never come back. That will never come back. I'm not saying if it was wrong or right. But guess what? That was my job. I had to do it."

That's one reason why when the orders came in for DC, it didn't take long for Lagares-Gomez to share the news of his new assignment with his family. A short time later, he found himself on a trip with then-President Bill Clinton to New York.

"My dad used to live in New York. He passed away a couple of years ago. I told him we were coming. He asked if he could meet the President. I said, 'I don't know.' I talked to the staff, and they said, no problem. So, they took all of his information and they put him in the rope line. The rope line is where he (the President) meets everybody and says hi.

"There were a lot of people there. So, I told my dad, look, stay right here. Whenever the President comes, they're gonna call you and then you're gonna take a picture with him. And my dad, he likes it. He was funny. I told him, don't be funny. Don't do anything stupid.

"So, I later received a call from the Secret Service. They said, 'Hey Ivan, the President wants to see you.' I wasn't at the event. I was upstairs doing some work at the hotel. I didn't know what had happened to my dad. I got scared. I was sweating as I came down.

"I look at my dad and he was hugging the President. And the President goes, 'Ivan, Is this your dad?'

"I said, 'yes sir.'

"The President (Clinton) said, 'oh my God, this guy is so funny. He's amazing. He is my amigo.' So, they took a picture together."

Lagares-Gomez served the Office of the President across two administrations, the Clinton Administration and the Bush Administration. Even though there were differences, he said the primary goal was always to not fail.

"You always have to get the mission done. There's no red or blue. There's not. There's a lot of stuff that happens behind the curtains that people don't realize, especially on an overseas trip. So much money, equipment, security, logistics to get the job done. Because it's a no-fail."

The concept of no-fail was never more apparent than in the work Lagares-Gomez did in support of President Clinton's Middle East Peace Summit in July of 2000. Held at Camp David, it was the latest effort of its kind to end the Israeli-Palestinian Conflict. Palestinian Chairman Yasser Arafat along with Israeli Prime Minister Ehud Barak as well their staffs met for several days at the secluded Presidential Retreat.

"I remember when we were down at Camp David. I spent days with both the Israelis and the Palestinians. In the sessions, they had one group on one side and the other on the other side. It seemed they were about to fight just looking at each other. We couldn't choose sides. We just had to get the job done."

For his work at the Summit, Lagares-Gomez was recognized with the Joint Service Achievement Medal. That medal is awarded by the Secretary of Defense for what is called achievement with distinction. It's considered an important award and somewhat rare since it's an award that's not exclusive to any one branch. In the case of Lagares-Gomez, it was received for providing support to the President during this important conference.

While the Summit didn't produce any agreements, the two sides agreed to keep discussions going, no minor achievement during those troubled times. A short time later, however, a new Intifada or what became known as the second Palestinian Uprising derailed those efforts.

Another one of those overseas trips brought Lagares-Gomez to India as he flew ahead of the President to make sure everything had been buttoned down. This role is considered critical because once the President arrives, especially on foreign soil, there shouldn't be any surprises.

"I flew with the 'car plane.' It was a C-5 cargo plane full of the limos that the President would need. We landed in Guam and changed to a pair of C-17s for the 12-hour trip to India. Altogether, we were in the air for more than 20 hours with two in-air refuelings. There's a lot of turbulence because there's a plane on top of you. So, you can get bounced around pretty good and a lot of people get sick."

That trip, in March of 2000, was the first by a sitting U.S. President to India in more than 20 years. President Jimmy Carter had last visited in 1978. During the session, President Clinton met that country's president. They signed a joint statement on energy and the environment.

The U.S. President also had the rare privilege of addressing the Indian Parliament. Reports at the time said the normally stoic members of Parliament rose in thunderous applause after the address.

The visit was widely seen as a turning point in Indo-U.S. ties. It was a time of great concern about nuclear proliferation and here, it was the President who walked a fine line when asked if India should ratify the nuclear test ban treaty.

Mister Clinton recognized the fact that the United States had also not ratified it and said it wasn't his place to tell India what to decide. That decision won him respect throughout the country.

During his visit to the region, President Clinton also became the first U.S. leader to visit nearby Bangladesh. He met with that country's Prime Minister and laid a wreath at a monument honoring those killed in Bangladesh's war of Independence in 1971. For Lagares-Gomez, just getting to Bangladesh was an adventure in itself.

"We were on the way to Bangladesh and the route took us close to Mount Everest. The pilot told us that if you open your window on the left side, you can see Mount Everest. The pilot actually made a U-turn and went around twice because some people were sleeping. I didn't have a camera, but yeah, I saw it.

"We spent the day in Bangladesh and later we went to Pakistan. That was a little different too, because, you know, India and Pakistan, not exactly the best friends. I remember when we went there, we went to this town. There was nobody on the street. It was like a ghost town. It was a quick one there. I think he only did it because he went to India. He had to be there too."

The President also made a brief detour to Geneva before returning home where he met with President Hafez al-Assad of Syria. It was an effort to restart the peace talks between Israel and Syria. The surprise session was the third face-to-face session of Clinton's Presidency, but while the two men talked for more than three hours, nothing concrete came out of those discussions.

White House Press Secretary Joe Lockhart later told reporters that the President wasn't disappointed. "It involves tough issues," said Lockhart. "So, I don't think the President leaves here anything but glad that, at the end of this trip, he was able to have this face-to-face meeting with President Assad."

President Clinton was one to change up schedules if he thought he could make it work, Lagares-Gomez said. That meant that at times, he was late. Lagares-Gomez said that changed significantly when George W. Bush became President.

"So, the first year, I think we were going to Ohio. Half of the staff got left behind because President Bush was early. And that was his story, if he wasn't on time, he was early."

President Bush was also known as an avid runner and ran frequently while at his ranch in Waco. Lagares-Gomez was one of those who participated in what they called the "heat run." To make the run, it must be 102 degrees or better.

"So, what they do is tell people, the 'heat run' is today. It's usually three miles long through his ranch. If you finish with him, then you get a picture with him. It was hard. If you aren't used to running in that heat, you are going to suffer. There were some Marines who tried to keep up with him and they ended up with IVs in their arms.

"I finished, but oh, my God, I was down for a couple of days. But the President, he did this frequently. He used to spend the whole month of August in his ranch."

Lagares said no matter how the world saw the Presidents he served, to him they were just people and the Presidents saw him the same way. That was exemplified in a story about his first encounter with President George H.W. Bush.

"The first time I met President (George H.W.) Bush 41, I was taking luggage to the residence. I was sitting it down and he looked at me and told me to come over here and sit down. I had stuff to do, but you can't tell him no. So, we talked for about ten or fifteen minutes, which is a long, long time. And then, (President George W.) Bush 43 came in and asked what I was doing. I didn't really know him that well at the time and he asked, 'what are you doing with my dad?' And that's who he was. We talked a long, long time. 41 said "I really enjoyed our conversation. Thank you for your service. If's there anything I can do for you let me know!'

"I said, 'I'm a huge baseball fan. Can you sign a baseball me for me?' And he said 'Yes! yes.'

"So, I went back and finished what I was doing but I came back to him with a baseball. He (41) signed it and then tossed it to 43 and said, 'sign that for Ivan.' And he (43) looked at me, like you know, what are you doing? I thought I was going to get fired, but he (43) signed it 'To Ivan, best wishes.'"

Baseball was a part of America's healing process after September 11th. White House aides had pushed for President Bush to throw out the first pitch of Game One of the World Series in Arizona, arguing such a move would be safer in terms of security. But the President rebuffed them. He was determined to throw out 'his' first pitch at Yankee Stadium in New York City, not far from where the Twin Towers of the World Trade Center once stood.

When he arrived at Yankee Stadium, the Secret Service gave the President a bulletproof vest which he wore under his jacket with the FDNY (Fire Department of New York) logo. Bush wasn't a fan of the vest, but he knew why it was needed.

As the President warmed up out of sight of the gathering crowd, Yankee Captain Derek Jeter greeted him. "Don't bounce it," Jeter said. "They'll boo you."

Minutes later, President Bush took the mound to applause and loud cheers of "U-S-A, U-S-A." Then, the former sports legend in Texas fired a perfect strike across the plate.

The healing had begun.

CHAPTER 3

Eighteen Acres

Rob Cole, Presidential Service Badge #19620

Photo of Rob Cole and his sons at the White House (Photo courtesy: Rob Cole)

The White House is a place at the center of our collective history. It's not just the home of the President. In many ways, it's the heart of our democracy. And when those eighteen acres that make up the White House Complex are decorated in their holiday-finest, it becomes more than a special place, it becomes a magical one.

It wasn't always that way. Historians tell us the first White House Christmas Party was held in 1800 when President John Adams and First Lady Abigail Adams hosted a party for their four-year-old granddaughter Susanna Boylston Adams.

Nearly a century later, in 1889, President Benjamin Harrison and his family gathered around the first White House Christmas tree in the second-floor oval room. It was decorated with candles. Electricity would come to the White House two years later and the first electrical lights were used in 1894, during the Presidency of Grover Cleveland.

In 1923, President Calvin Coolidge was the first Chief Executive to mark the season with the lighting of the National Christmas Tree.

For Navy Commander Rob Cole (Presidential Service Badge #19620), these historical notes were part of the lore surrounding the world's most famous address.

"Christmas at the White House was always amazing. I mean take your top ten Christmases that you've ever seen of just whatever, decorations and what not, at least for me, and put them all together. That's what it was like. There's a picture that I have with Spot and Barney, and if you look in the background, that's actually where you can see they were bringing in the poinsettias. They had a poinsettia Christmas tree. So, it was 100 percent live poinsettias. They were arranged in the shape of a Christmas tree. That's the kind of stuff that you saw when you went from room to room in some of the public spaces. There's no phony greenery. It's all real. It all came from somewhere. That just really adds to the ambience and the beauty of it all."

It wasn't just the Christmas holiday that Cole was able to share with his family and friends.

"We were fortunate as White House staff to be able to come and watch the Washington DC fireworks from the South Lawn of the White House. That was a pretty special time."

Those lighter moments helped balance the stress of the work he did in support of the Office of the President. In fact, many weekends, on his off time, he gave tours of the White House to friends and family.

"I just felt that the real treat, other than the professional aspect, was to be able to share that. I felt so lucky and blessed to be able to share the White House with the people closest to me. It was just nice. If there was nothing going on, I could actually take people into the Situation Room Conference Room. That's the room where all of the photo ops happened. That's where everyone comes to meet for classified briefings. But it's only a small portion of the actual situation room. The rest is also a secure facility where the National Security Advisor's office is located. It's the nerve center for everything that's happening on the 'classified' side of the Office of the President."

Cole also spent time on tours of his own. His clearance allowed him access to all parts of the building. A self-professed history buff, there was a time when he found a somewhat rare artifact.

"The staff knows about it but there's a spot under the North Portico that has not been renovated or repainted since the White House was burned by the British in 1814. The soot marks are still there. It's in a true working spot of the White House, a spot you would never see on television. Just to know that the history of that building goes back, well over 200 years, that's just really amazing.

"I was sharing with my wife, and she was, 'wow, it really makes you wonder what else is there?' You know that the building has been built up, so many things have been built around it through the years.

What is really in the heart of that original wall so to speak? It really does make you wonder."

Cole arrived at the White House in May 2002 from the Naval Air Systems Command at Patuxent River, Maryland. He had spent his career in the Navy, serving on the USS Finback as well as the USS Enterprise. He later enrolled in the Naval Post-Graduate school where he became proficient in Contracting and Financial Management. This specialty called for getting the most of out of every dollar and ensuring that his units had what they needed to fulfill the mission. When he was initially approached about the position at the White House, he thought it would be great if he got an interview, just so he could see the building. Later, he told his family his dream was reality.

"Hey, I got an interview at the White House," he told them. "I know, we've been talking about doing a lot of things, what would you guys think about if I got a job at the White House? Oh, man, okay, if it was only that easy. But I was, I was very fortunate to be able to get that job and spend a couple of years serving at the White House. It's the only place that I've ever worked, that just arriving at work each day was just a treat. I would have been happy to just come to work to be the janitor and take the trash out every day because you got to go to the White House. You walk onto the White House grounds, and it's unbelievable."

Serving at the White House, and especially for the Office of the President, is not an easy job. In many positions at many different organizations, people are focused on themselves and looking out for themselves. At the White House, Cole said his colleagues served a different purpose, a solitary purpose: The Mission.

"Failure is absolutely not an option. I mean, there are probably plenty of things in life and in the world where failure is a stepping-stone, but not there. My second director at the Situation Room actually summed it up pretty well. He said, 'We want to be on the leading edge of everything, but we don't want to be on the bleeding edge.' He said when you get to the bleeding edge, that's where failure might happen because you're dealing with unproven scenarios or whatever. You want to be on the leading edge of things, but you don't want to be so far out there that you are alone."

As a Navy Commander, he felt that pressure, especially in the days after September 11.

"It was a fairly tense period of time, all through our country. We had all sorts of personal protective equipment in our office. I really did sit around the office one day thinking, 'I wonder if we should get a really good bottle of whiskey when they say to put this stuff on so we could crack open that bottle and enjoy our last moments together.'"

Cole had a number of duties in the White House Situation Room, but his primary task was the business side of things. In short, he was responsible for making sure the President and his staff had all the technology and equipment they needed to do their jobs. Running the day-to-day operations included caring, not only for the technology, but ensuring that the support staff of the Situation Room were focused and on mission. Of course, there were also some collateral, unplanned duties.

"I like to say my favorite claim to fame is the day we bombed Iraq is that I was getting water for the Joint Chiefs of Staff. Yes, I was the water boy for the day. I was happy to do it.

"It's kind of funny and we can certainly chuckle about it, but that's what I was doing. The tension was as thick as anything I'd ever felt. You could just feel it in the air and from everybody. It's stressful, but we are all professionals. We have our act together. Nobody lost control."

One thing that many people might not know is the standard for Presidential Records. Recordings were not allowed, something that dates back to the Watergate era. Even so, there had to be a permanent record of every official Presidential phone call. There was a day when Cole found himself on the line with President George W. Bush and an unnamed foreign leader.

"The President had gone through a 60-second monologue introducing topics and other items when someone came on the line to say the line had been lost. Bush responded, 'Gosh darn, let's get him back on!' We eventually did, but it just goes to show you that things can happen. If it was an English-to-English call, there weren't too many people listening in. However, if it was another language, you might have a lot of other people on the line. We would all literally listen to the call and take notes on what we heard. When it was over, everybody would take their notes into the Deputy Director of the Situation Room. He would piece them all together. I would say that his records were probably 99 percent accurate. That would then become the official record of the call.

"It is really a job that you never know what you're going to be doing on any given day. You might be taking notes from a Presidential call. You might be getting coffee or assisting whoever happens to be there. I felt like I and so many others who wore the uniform contributed."

Even now, more than a decade removed from his time at the White House, Cole still finds himself drawn back to his time at the Situation Room as he watches global events unfold from his home, both real and fictional.

"It's fun to watch any show that comes on and to see how they're portraying things and how it looks on television compared to real life. The one thing that I've noticed is, when you watch anything on television, the West Wing looks like a large office building. It's actually quite small. The hallways are quite tight. It's an old building and most of the President's staff doesn't have an office in the West Wing itself."

For Cole, this place is more than just the eighteen acres and the people who work there. It's a symbol of what our country can be, of what we can be, if we only allow ourselves to do so.

"I left the White House in 2004, so many years ago. And in those years, I've never found that (sense of a singular purpose) again. It seems that there are a lot of times when it only takes one person to think 'it's about me,' and it kind of changes the whole dynamic of everything. (What we had) is extremely rare.

"You know, just walking through the hallways of the White House and just realizing the kind of things that went on in history and things that everybody knows about, let alone the stuff that people don't know about, it really is remarkable. It's just a great place to work from any perspective, let alone the history that you see and feel when you walk through the hallways. You realize the kind of things that went on throughout history."

Being a Presidential Service Badge Recipient, in Cole's eyes, is an honor.

"It's really an acknowledgement that you served the people of the United States and the Office of the President in a really meaningful way.

"It's an honor to be part of that fraternity, that family, and to have had the opportunity to do that service. One of the really nice things at the White House was—I was a Navy Commander. My boss was an Admiral. We had enlisted people. We had all people of all different ranks in the military—but at the White House, we never got caught up in any of that. It was really just a place where people came and did their service together, and everybody was on the same team.

"You get used to the pace of things, but it is still pretty overwhelming. If you were to take a step back and try to think of it as if you're in the middle of it, you would actually say, 'Oh, my gosh! How does anybody keep up?' But you just do it because that's what has to be done.

"I think, if I recall correctly, I was the seventeenth person interviewed just for my job. I don't know if I was the best or the brightest. But I remember the Chief of Staff (Andrew Card) kicking off a meeting one day. I can't exactly paraphrase what he said, but it was something like, 'We at the White House get the best and the brightest.' So, it's kind of amazing, the people you work with, and the people that come through here and serve.

"We would help each other out on weekends. We would get together. I think because you have been through such intense situations together, you form a bond that sticks forever. We had the opportunity to do some pretty exciting, some pretty neat things. We'll always have that to fall back on, but the trust and the competence of the people you are working with. You know that they are always going to be there for you.

"The White House just brings that to a different level. You're up at the organization that helps set the policy for everybody else doing things there in the world. From a military perspective, it can be overwhelming, but again, the location is just amazing. When you step inside the 18 acres, it's just a whole different world. I think that really makes it a special place to serve and know that you're doing things that are going to make the world a better place. That's what we're all striving for, to make the world a little bit better, a little bit safer."

CHAPTER 4

My dad told me, "You are not coming home"

Jonée Coleman, Presidential Service Badge #22353

President Barack Obama poses for a photograph with Jonee' Coleman at the White House Oval Office, (Photo courtesy: Jonee' Coleman)

They say there's nothing like a father's love for his daughter. That was certainly true for Joe Coleman, Jr. A life-long computer engineer and educator in the city of Anderson, Indiana; Joe knew that for his daughter, Jonée Coleman, to reach her potential, she would have to do it away from home.

"Time was winding down and my enlistment was coming to an end," she said. "I had to make the life-altering decision of whether I was going to re-enlist or get out. I was really missing home at the time and my mother was working her magic to make the decision of my childhood home all the more enticing.

"She said things like, 'Oh, you can always come home,' and 'I can take care of you.' Those invitations sounded so endearing, warm, and loving. On the other hand, I remember my dad saying, 'No! Don't you come home.'"

Jonée's father knew that, while she could easily walk into a job with one of the General Motors (GM) plants back home and work alongside him, he didn't want her to come back. He said, "You have opportunities out there."

"He said, 'If you choose to come back home, it's your choice but don't let anyone else influence you.'"

Coleman would find out years later that deep down inside, he did want her back home, but he knew that it wouldn't have been the best decision for her life. The whole experience rocked her. She remembered asking him one last time, 'So, you don't want me to come back, even to work?'

"He said, 'No, because I love you.'

"I knew that he would rather have me continue on my own path and for me to live my life the way I saw fit. He was willing to sacrifice that time with me and cut the umbilical cord so that I could stand and fight on my own two feet. His advice meant the world to me because he always recognized something in me that I hadn't yet seen in myself. It was a short time later when I received military orders to the White House. I remember calling him and my mom crying because I was overwhelmed with what was happening. My mom was a bit disappointed that I wasn't coming home because she is very loving and very protective quite naturally. My father understood my mother's love for me, and I think that is why he had to make the call, even if it hurt everyone involved."

Joe Coleman, Jr. passed away in 2018, but he was able to see his daughter achieve her dream and answered prayer of being in the White House.

"I had a very close relationship with both parents, but in different ways. When it came to him, it was special. He used to speak a great deal using metaphors and could create powerful visions with the usage of his words. He could talk politics, analyze any sporting event, while simultaneously rocking babies, playing with toddlers, and empathizing while speaking comfort and encouragement to anyone who was hurting or in pain. That's what I miss the most about him. He could speak to me in such a way that I could completely understand. His metaphors and analogies are what kept me going throughout my military career and still influence me (and others) to this day."

In her time at the White House, from January 2006 to November 2010, Staff Sergeant Jonée Coleman (Presidential Service Badge #22353) worked with two different administrations, each with their own ideas of how to govern. However, day in and day out, Coleman had no doubt that she was where she was supposed to be. After all, she envisioned this calling many years ago while she was a young girl growing up amongst the cornfields of rural Indiana.

"I remember having this vision like it was yesterday. I was hanging out in my brother's room on a warm summer day. I must have been nine or ten years old. He was sitting on the bottom edge of his waterbed playing his video game that was on the dresser in front of him. I was on the opposite corner at the head of the waterbed, lying on my back with my feet propped up against the wall. I don't know if you would call it a premonition or something, but I remember asking my brother, 'Where do you see yourself going when you grow up?' He paused the video game and looked over his shoulder at me. He didn't say anything. It was just the look he gave me, like 'what?' After a moment, he asked the same question that his face expressed.

"I told him that I felt like I was supposed to go to Washington DC. He stared at me and said, 'okay…' He turned back and started playing his video game again. Although Mario and the Goombah's captured my brother's attention at the time, I just kept right on talking and said, 'I don't know how I'm going to get there, and I don't know when, but I'm going.' At this time, I saw what looked like tiny little footprints going up the wall from where my feet were positioned. They stopped on a star a little way up the wall, just under the wainscoting. Then, a circle surrounded the little feet on the star. After that, a map of the entire DC metropolitan area appeared under the star, and that is when I realized that the footprints stopped at the nation's capital. I whispered to myself again, 'I'm going there one day.'"

Coleman arrived at The White House after more than five years with the U.S. Army as an Information Systems Operator-Analyst. She was responsible for making sure classified and unclassified systems and operations functioned for those who needed them. It was a role that she took very seriously and handled quite well at her other duty stations. In her last position at Fort Gordon, Coleman served in the Command Group under the installation's first female general, Brigadier General (BG) Janet Hicks (Ret.). Coleman was the general's personal information assurance security officer (IASO) and provided support to the top officials on post. However, to be asked to serve at the White House Communications Agency was an entirely different level of responsibility. Even being considered for that kind of position was something that only a small number of military personnel received.

"The interview process for the position at the White House was in itself quite an ordeal. If you are able to make it through the initial round, that's already saying something about you as a person. That's because the investigators are not only talking to you. They're talking to other people about you. They are trying to assess your character. They want to know who you are from various points of view and if the viewpoints are consistent.

"Yes, you can share who you are, but they take into consideration what other people say about you, and rightfully so. I mean this office is not one you can just apply for and walk through the door. You can't just sign up down the street or at another military installation. This position represents the face of the Presidency. Whether you are out in public or you are operating behind the scenes, you are still representing that office."

Like those who walk along Pennsylvania Avenue and appear awestruck when looking from the street into the White House compound, Coleman found herself dealing with similar emotions when she walked through the gate for the first time. She soon realized that there wasn't time to merely "look around." She had to get to work.

"I wasn't too nervous initially. Suddenly, my nerves gave in, and it hit me: This is real. This is big. When you put on a military uniform, you already know that you are serving something bigger than yourself. When you walk into that environment (The White House), the weight of who you represent is actually overwhelming. You instinctively understand what that means when you cross that threshold."

Even though she worked for two different administrations, Coleman perceived that she was required to be unbiased in her mannerism while serving the Office of the President.

"We may have held certain beliefs and preferred personal preferences, but it all comes down to the mission. We were all professional and we respected each other. I'm not saying that we were always perfect and that tensions didn't build from time to time behind closed doors. However, the majority of the time, we may only have one shot to accomplish a successful mission, so no matter what, we maintained professionalism and respect because so many lives and careers depended on us. As for the mission, there were no opportunities to say, 'Oh well, we will get it right next time.'"

Like so many others who served at the White House, Coleman recognized that her position was a high-stress, crisis-oriented environment, largely because of what was at stake. When you serve the leader of the free world, you must be laser focused on what's happening at the time. You also must be prepared for what may come next.

"You have to learn to let go of things quickly because it can have an impact on what you're doing at the moment, and that could also impact something else in the future."

Coleman worked on both travel and fixed missions. In serving on each side, she admitted having an appreciation for the challenges and goals of each but learned a lot from both.

"It was great to serve in both capacities. There were some hard times and some growing pains to boot, just like with anything in life. In the (White House Communications) agency, you have to be ready to go at all times. The environment was not 'if the call comes but when the call comes.' Sometimes you think or feel you knew the gravity of a situation, then an unforeseen situation or circumstance happened, and you had to pivot and go."

That "pivot and go" mentality is something that Coleman recognized heavily during her time at the White House. It's also something that she's carried with her in her daily life. "It helped me to be able to look at an issue and say, 'Okay, this is a challenge, but this is how I am going to accomplish it.' You make decisions and at the time, you think they are right, but sometimes they are not. Then, you may tell yourself, 'I could have done this or that better.' The truth is that we are all human and we all make mistakes. That's part of the growth process. You're not going to be 100 percent correct or 100 percent right all of the time. However, I've learned a lot from each and every decision."

Those decisions included several travel missions where the team operated in what she called "hidden in plain sight." Or so she thought at one event.

"We were at one location, and the team and I went to grab something to eat. As we're leaving our worksite, there's a reporter standing nearby asking passing pedestrians questions. We were all surprised, but we had to act fast. So, as soon as we turned the corner, we made some calls."

When you are working with the president, there is a certain level of secrecy that needs to be maintained, both for his safety and for those of the team. It's important to be hidden, yet accessible for those who need you to be.

"I'm not exactly sure how the information got out about what the reporter thought we were doing, but we had to change a huge part of the mission. It's not like the reporter was doing anything wrong. He was just doing his job. However, due to the optics, we had to change up a large part of our operations quickly.

"I remember that many people were upset about it. I understood why. However, my point of view was 'This is what we do.' It was just amazing to see how fast we were able to pivot and go."

On the travel missions, Coleman had a chance to see others in the world up close, and in doing so, she came away with a greater appreciation for her own life.

"When you head overseas, you have a rare chance to experience cultures that you never dreamt of seeing, of visiting places that you never dreamt of going. I think that being around different types of people who were just happy and content, even though they had nowhere near the resources or opportunities of others, well, it just warmed my heart."

Coleman moved from travel to fixed missions largely because of the physical demands and stress. She also felt that "staying home" was more conducive to her private life.

"That transition to fixed missions from travel took a lot of adjustment and self-reflection. Initially, I was not happy about it but in the end, I was grateful because I didn't realize how much my body needed that break. The transition also really helped me grow. I took on more of a leadership position, which benefitted me then and is still benefiting me to this day."

Coleman recognized there is a duty that comes with serving the White House. It's not just that people from all walks of life that enter with the goal of just serving, but to serve a common mission together with each other for so many others.

"One thing that I was absolutely inspired by was our unity. You may not know who everyone is, but everyone knows what the mission is. You know how it's going to get done. Would I do it again? Absolutely! There's nothing like it in the world. To look back on it and say that I was part of something historical. It's pretty awesome. We are just like other members of the military, but we just did something a little different. It's about making that difference to show that people can work together, regardless."

Ironically, her last day at the White House was also her last day in an Army uniform. Even so, it wasn't her last day at "Eighteen Acres"—the insider's term for the White House Complex.

"I left the White House and the military, but within a month, I was back there as a civilian contractor. I was now serving in a different mission. I had a different role, without the military uniform. It was definitely a change. Quite a change, actually. Both mentally and psychologically, the shift in thinking played a major part in how I viewed myself. I understood that although the mission may have changed, the singularity of purpose was still there."

It's that focus that drives Coleman today. She readily admits that she will complete whatever "mission" God has in store for her. The mission-focused mindset is what led her to the Dog Tag Fellowship Program.

Based in Washington, D.C., Dog Tag Inc. (DTI) is a non-profit that helps veterans, military spouses and caregivers find new goals and challenges. Through an immersive five-month fellowship program, those who take part can gain first-hand experience in professional development, entrepreneurship, team building, and project management while simultaneously taking college courses with Georgetown University. Upon completion of the program, fellows will receive a business certification from the School of Continuing Studies from Georgetown University along with life skills, a mentor, a dynamic network of alumni, and access to the fellowship's partners that can help put the fellows on a path to success. That path and purpose is important to make sure that veterans and military spouses can re-enter their communities with the confidence and support they need to succeed. That bridge is key and one reason why Coleman believes DTI is yet another chance for her to make a difference.

"Some people think that the military uniform is just another uniform. Well, it's not just a uniform or just another uniform; it's an identity that many associate themselves with. When you take it off, it's like a superhero taking off his cape and asking, 'Who am I now?'

"Now, you have to actually speak about yourself, who you are outside of the uniform. There is no more cape, no more uniform, no more awards. For many transitioning service members, communicating, let alone knowing who we are when the uniform is no longer present can be quite a challenge. That's why having access to training programs during that transition is so important.

"Having the ability to access quality transition classes can cut down on some of the anxiety and depression associated with the new lifestyle. To be able to speak about these challenges is really speaking not only to the change in physical requirements that are going to take place, but to the psychological aspects, implications, and toll that the transition process has on servicemembers is very important and under-researched. For many, going through the transition process is a mental health challenge in itself. The thought of even wearing civilian attire on a regular basis can be a huge transition and undertaking that can impact the service member and their family, which can also impact many other things such as employment, promotions, and their overall livelihood."

"Every service member is going to have to go through their transition at some point and time, no matter their age, rank, where they enlisted or if they were commissioned or not. There comes a day when everyone in the military will cycle out. So, why not make the transition as easy, informative, consistent throughout every branch, and as hopeful as possible?"

Coleman is currently pursuing her master's degree in psychology with a concentration in Industrial and Organizational Psychology. She's also working as a graduate research assistant with HELM Wholeness Community Services. With her years of education and experience as an image consultant and Veteran, she is actively pursuing a grant for further research on the physical and psychological implications of image and fashion on the transitioning service member.

Joe Coleman, Jr. envisioned his daughter's success away from home. Jonée Coleman honored her father's vision for her success by answering the call to serve at the White House instead of giving in to the longing of wanting to come home.

CHAPTER 5

You're a part of history

Jeff Worthington, Presidential Service Badge #27034

Jeff Worthington, who was commander of the 2d Theatre Signal Brigade in Europe, meets with Lt. Gen. Steven Fogarty, ARCYBER Commander discussing the expansion of communications in Eastern Europe (Poland) as well as the Black Sea region. (Photo from Jeff Worthington)

"Everyone wants to know that they're doing something good. Maybe that's it. It taps into the psyche of a person. There's not many of you. You know your role and you know that you are enabling the President to do what needs to be done. You can read something and know that you were inside the room when he met with President Karzai or when they talk about the trip to Moscow, you know you ate dinner at (Russian President Vladimir) Putin's house when the President was there. Everyone likes the fact that they were part of something like that, something that made a difference."

For Colonel Jeff Worthington (U.S. Army, Ret.) every day he served at the White House was a day full of memories.

"I would tell you it (the days) didn't matter. I would love to know what other people say. For me, it didn't matter whether it was the first time or the 50th time, when I walked onto 'Eighteen Acres,' it felt the same. Every time you walked on there, you walked through the metal detectors, and you gave them your badge and your ID, you walk past all of the people looking through the fence line on the South Lawn.

"I remember vividly. You are talking to yourself and telling yourself that you cannot believe that you are walking into the White House. Whether it was the first time or it was the 10th time or it was the 30th, it was like that every time. You wonder if you're going to wake up from a dream because it's an amazing opportunity. You're walking down the halls of the White House, and no one is stopping you. No one is telling you that you shouldn't be here. No one is wondering what you are doing. You are a part of the White House. It's weird. It's very hard to explain.

"There's just so much history and tradition. Did you know that in front of the White House in the basement, as you walk out of where the kitchen is, there's still black soot, above the door frames from the War of 1812? I mean, that's what amazing history you are walking through and a small part of without even thinking about it. There are just so many stories that most Americans will never hear. For example, President Richard Nixon covered the swimming pool and made it the Press Briefing Room because he didn't like the unflattering photographs that they took of him from the old Briefing Room. And underneath the floor, you can still walk inside the old, unfilled pool. You can sign your name on the inside of the pool that Nixon swam in. I think that's why it is, there's so much there that you're a part of."

It's not just the history and tradition, it's the reverence of the institution itself that is clearly felt from serving at the White House. Even so, Worthington (Presidential Service Badge #27034) said there was work to be done and there was no time to be a "tourist."

"I believed in the way and what President (George W.) Bush said about the White House. He always came into the Oval Office in a coat and tie. He never had anything else on other than a coat and tie. Because it was the respect and reverence. I'm paraphrasing that. He showed the office, the Office of the President that respect. So, whenever I was in the White House, I tried to emulate that. I wanted to respect the Executive Office of the President that I was supporting."

Worthington came to the White House after an already-accomplished career in the Army. During that time, he got to know General Stanley McChrystal, his battalion commander in the 82nd Airborne Division. McChrystal was his Battalion and later his Joint Special Operations Command (JSOC) Commander while assigned to the Joint Communications unit for four years. It was a relationship that changed Worthington's career trajectory in ways even he never foresaw.

The relationship led Worthington to shift to the Signal Corps. The United States Army Signal Corps (USASC) was formed in 1860. Developed by Major Albert Myer, it initially served the Union Army.

Its first test in combat came in June of 1861 as battery fire was directed at Confederate positions. It later evolved to include aerial surveillance and even a telegraph train. Tucked into the organization in 1870 was the beginning of something quite familiar to everyone who watches for dangerous storms: the National Weather Service. Today, USASC creates and manages communications to support the command and control of all U.S. Armed Forces. In short, any message that needs to get from A to B, the USASC provides oversight.

Ironically, the Signal Corps is the mother of the Air Force. They were the first aviators, even before there was the Army Air Corps. In fact, the Army Air Corps were born out of Signal Corps pilots.

For someone who had been in Infantry, being in the Signal Corps was a dramatic change. However, Worthington said had he not moved there, he would never have made it to the White House or been presented with many of the opportunities he had during his career.

"I was going to fight moving to the Signal Corps. I didn't want to do it. He (McChrystal) told me in his office one day, and I'll remember this forever, that 'you need to go down there and be the best signal officer that you possibly can be.' He challenged me to be the best I could be in Signal. And so, I went over there and really enjoyed it. I never would have had the opportunity (at the White House) that I had, had he not encouraged me to stick with it and stay in the Signal Corps and in the Army.

"I got to work for him again when he was commander of the Joint Special Operations Command. I was in one of the subordinate organizations in JSOC. So, I worked for him then and learned how, and why, Senior Leaders make many of the decisions they do. I learned how to handle adversity, success, and challenges. It was a lesson in leadership that formed much of what I am today.

"I have a deep respect for General McChrystal. He is one of the leaders that taught me how to lead but be humble. How to provide purpose and direction, but not over-exert your influence. So, I really do like General McChrystal. He built a great coalition inside JSOC.

"He had such respect and trust from those across the Battalion (2-504 PIR) that we knew he would always look out for us ... and we would look out for him. I used to joke that if General McChrystal, then Lieutenant Colonel McChrystal told you to walk to the third floor to the roof and jump off, you would. It was not blind obedience, but rather an understanding that you knew he would take care of you, and you never wanted to disappoint him or your men."

That support of, and respect for McChrystal was forged, literally, in fire. Worthington was at Fort Bragg during the so-called "Green Ramp" tragedy. On March 23, 1994, an F-16 collided with a C-130 Hercules Transport in the skies over Pope Air Force Base in North Carolina. The C-130 eventually landed safely, but the F-16 did not. As the F-16 crew ejected, the aircraft continued toward an area known as "Green Ramp," a place well-known to those on the base. Lying on the western end of the East-West runway, it was a common staging area for joint exercises involving the Army and the Air Force. The disintegrating F-16 hit the ground. The debris narrowly missed a pair of C-130s on the ground but cartwheeled into a parked C-141. Fuel tanks were punctured, sending a huge fireball and wreckage into the area where 500 paratroopers had gathered moments earlier as part of their training activities for the day.

At the time of the accident, half of Worthington's battalion was at the rifle range, while the other half were jumping in that day's joint training exercise. He had sent one of his Specialists (SPCs) to jump because he had missed one earlier that week. When the accident happened, Worthington, who was a few miles away, could see the plumes of dark black smoke. The range was immediately shut down and he headed back to headquarters to await word of what happened. It was the first time that he had lost someone in his command.

"I actually had one SSG (Staff Sergeant) who was at Jumpmaster school. He survived because someone yelled 'jump' and they all jumped between the CONNEXes (Shipping Containers)—protecting them from the fireball. They then went to aid others, taking the time to get the fire extinguishers from the waiting HMMWVs (Humvees). Unfortunately, the extinguishers were the wrong kind for the currently used fuel in the F-16 and did little to reduce the flames."

The stench of fuel was strong. That fuel coated many of the paratroopers, making it even more challenging to render aid. The smell of burning flesh was everywhere. Survivors later spoke of how much the scene reminded them of the horrors of actual warfare.

Here is a radio transcript of that fateful crash:

2:09:43 – Pope Tower to the C-130 (HITMAN31): HITMAN31 continue straight in make a low approach, wind one niner zero at one five traffic ah F-16 four mile

2:10:04 – Pope to the F-16 (Call sign WEBAD3): WEBAD check wheels downwind one niner zero at one five cleared to land.

2:10:07 – F-16 to Pope: WEBAD3 three green... low approach

2:10:16 – Pope to C-130: HITMAN31 ah present position right closed approved

2:10:20 – C-130 to Pope: Present position right closed for 31 wilco

2:10:26 – UNKNOWN: (background noise) ... J***s

2:10:30 – UNKNOWN: (background noise) ... Oh s**t; Holy s**t

2:10:32 – UNKNOWN: Tower you got that midair?

2:10:34 – UNKNOWN: Tower we had a midair collision, midair, midair
2:10:36 – UNKNOWN: Eject, eject, get out of there, get out of there
2:10:38 – UNKNOWN: There he goes
2:10:39 – UNKNOWN: We got an ejection
2:10:43 – UNKNOWN: Got two chutes
2:10:48 – UNKNOWN: Tower there's a big ***Garbled***
2:10:50 – Pope: Fayetteville Pope, the runway's closed, oh my God!
(Courtesy: The Military Times)

In what would become the worst loss of life for the 82nd Airborne since World War II, 23 paratroopers were killed. More than 100 others were hurt. One other passed a year later. Then-Lieutenant Colonel Stanley McChrystal commanded one of the battalions of paratroopers. Then-Lieutenant Colonel Lloyd Austin, who would later serve as Secretary of Defense in the Biden Administration, commanded the other. Both received high marks for how they handled the disaster and how they helped their men to recover. It was something that Worthington, who was serving under McChrystal at the time, saw first-hand.

"There is no greater test of a leader than to lead in a time of great suffering and sorrow. I saw just the steadfast leadership here. He had very calm, stalwart leadership. He got us all back into an airplane, jumping again, as soon as possible. Because he knew the longer we went not doing our job, the worse it was going to be. So, what I've tried to do is the same thing for the people that I serve. And I say, I serve. I don't mean the ones over me. I mean the ones who I technically outrank or are in charge of. So, it is very important. I will never think that

I had the same impact on anybody that General McChrystal had on me and the rest of the others, but I've tried my best to, to provide and lead by the same example. And to ensure that I develop the next crop of soldiers and leaders that are going to come after me, just like he did.

"He had an ability to make you mad at yourself. Mad to where you improved, rather than externalizing your anger at him or somebody else. That was very important. Because if you did something wrong and you were yelled at, it's easy to blame the person yelling at you. He never did that. So, you blame yourself, which I think made you work harder to be better.

"I've taken a quote from him, and I do take some poetic license with it. He's explained it to me two or three times. I can just never remember the whole thing. But I use it a lot. He would say, 'credibility brings freedom of maneuver.'

"So, the way I interpret that, as a signal leader, as a communicator, is if you establish the credibility with those that you are supporting, that you have their best interest at heart, that you're looking out for them, and you're always trying to get better for them, then when you get something wrong or make a mistake, they will forgive you. They will know that you didn't mean to do it. You're going to make sure that it doesn't happen again. Or, when you want to try something that is new and different. They know that you mean well, and they'll let you do it.

"He did that inside JSOC because we had to establish our credibility during the war. So that he could do what he needed to do because we relied on so many people to support us. I've kind of taken that and morphed it into me and tried to establish credibility with others that I support. I know we're going to mess something up. Something's going to happen. They need to know that we are going to be our own worst critic. We are going to make sure that we make it right for them. That's probably one of the biggest things that I took from him: Credibility brings freedom of maneuver."

Those lessons of leadership guided Worthington as he advanced in his military career, which included his time at the White House. However, there is also a darker side to the mantle of leadership that many are only now starting to notice, the challenge to excel despite the tremendous stress and pressure they are under. Some of that stress and pressure can be too much to bear, according to Worthington.

"We still have this stigma of what I'll call mental health or behavior health. We still have the stigma in the military that you, as a senior leader, can show no weakness."

Changing that paradigm is something that won't happen overnight because it's not just a military issue, it's a societal one. That said, military deaths by suicide have jumped dramatically in recent years as those serving our country deal with a multitude of issues common to many Americans including stress because of COVID. When you add those concerns to the stressors that come with life in the military, those who serve face additional burdens. It's not just the rank-and-file soldiers that are feeling the pressure, those general officers and senior leaders, like Colonel Worthington felt it as well.

"I remember the day that I said to myself, I know exactly why (our leaders) are committing suicide. There is the pressure of being more successful than you are already being told you are. Of what everyone thinks about you. They look up to you. Your family does. You're so successful. You can do so many things right. And then to do something wrong, although it may seem small, or you don't succeed. It may seem trivial to someone who has been that successful for that long. I can see exactly why it ends up the way it does."

Those words don't come easy for Worthington because he faced those same internal demons. There is a very real concern with some military leaders that even as they project a cool, calm aura, many feel they can't perform at the level that both their rank and their men and women expect. It was at Fort Bragg when Worthington made a decision that changed his life.

"I was at my desk one day as I was figuring out exactly what I was going to do and when and how. I was afraid to Google "military suicide family support" because I didn't want someone to look back and go 'he knew he was going to do this' and my family not receive any support or receive my death benefits.

"I said to myself, 'Holy Cow. This is when we tell our guys to go see someone about it.' We tell our guys to go get help. So, I walked over to the chaplain.

"Now, it's about an eighth of a mile from my office to the JSOC chaplain. I didn't know him at all. I would have felt more comfortable if it were someone that I knew, but I didn't. It (that walk) was very difficult. But what I kept thinking about was the alternative. I'm not around for my family and no one will take care of my family. What will people think about that?

"My family didn't even know what was going on because I was embarrassed to tell them that I was scared."

Worthington worked with Dr. Crystal Redding, a base psychologist. He credits her with helping in his recovery. It did take time, but the weight was lifted. His family, including his son, also helped to provide the support that Worthington needed.

"He had some problems adjusting when we were in Europe. So, he and I would to go his counseling sessions a couple of times a week. (When I shared my story with him and my wife), he said, 'I'm not losing my father to suicide, that is not going to happen.' So, he saw me filling some things out. And he said, 'Are you filling out the same sheet that I filled out when we were in Germany? I can help you fill those out if you want.'

"And so, my family supported me, and I didn't know they would. With Crystal (my psychologist) telling me: 'you're okay, you're not a bad person' and my family saying: 'how can we help you?' That's when it turned in a better direction.

"I do not know what would have happened, had I not met Crystal Redding. Everyone who is in a dark place in their life needs a Crystal Redding to lift them out into the light and help make them whole. For Crystal, there can be no amount of thanks that could repay the debt I owe you."

Worthington also used his rank to his advantage as he tried to raise awareness about the issue of mental health and the importance of what he called "decoupling" mental health from behavioral health.

"I think right now, we think, 'well, he's mentally ill.' He has problems. And that's not what it is at all. I am just having trouble. I need a personal trainer. You don't look at me poorly when I want to get stronger or want to lose weight. You don't say, 'he's got a weak body. He can never do anything.' So, why do we stigmatize efforts to make our brain stronger, to be mentally stronger? I just don't think that we're willing to take that jump off the diving board if you know what I mean."

As he continued to deal with his situation, Worthington found support, but also found some opposition. He went against the advice of some people he knew in the Army and attended behavioral health sessions at Fort Bragg dressed in his uniform. He wanted to have service members see a Colonel walk in there. He wanted people to say, "Well, I guess that's not bad. I guess we can go." Even today, Worthington says there's maintenance to be done.

"I've gotten in touch with Crystal a few times when it just hit me kind of hard. You see things on TV. I do have flashbacks of the whole thing. I relive the events leading up to my challenging times mostly when I am alone with time to think. Sometimes, it is just a flashback, a face, an email. But talking about it is therapeutic. When I talk about mistakes that I've made, it helps me get it off my chest and deal with it.

"I think we think that people feel that we have to be perfect all of the time and so, we put a lot of that pressure and stress on ourselves. I would tell you that people expect us to be perfect. You are being judged all the time. It can be stressful when you know that every word you say is being analyzed. So, you think about those things. You have to live up to all these things that people have said about you.

"I can handle combat. I can handle stress. I can handle combat support. I can be the one who hands the President the phone, and it's okay. This stress was very different. But I made the conscious decision, based on the strong leaders and similar situations that I had seen over my career, to make sure it did not consume me. To make sure it did not take over my life."

When it comes to phone calls, the phone call that helped to get Worthington to the White House was a call that he readily admits was a factor of luck and timing.

"I was in JSOC at the time and a friend of mine, Bill Burnham, had gone up to the White House from another JSOC unit. I loved my time there. I loved that we were doing something that mattered. That's very important to me. So, I was looking for something to do where I could be satisfied and also where I could continue being able to support something big.

"Now, off the record, I also knew that I needed to go to DC. And it was either on the east side of the Potomac or the west side of the Potomac. I felt that I could go to the Pentagon, but what an opportunity to be able to serve in the White House. So, I reached out to Bill

Burnham. I went for an interview and was selected. When I got the orders, my wife and I were extremely happy.

"You know, I used to tell my parents back in high school that I was going to be President one day. Now, my mom and I joke that—well, I didn't make President, but I supported the President. So, that was really just one degree of separation from my original goal back in 1987."

When one works at the White House, you are at the center of big decisions that happen almost daily. When those decisions happen, they are enabled by people like Colonel Worthington who was serving as the Presidential Response Officer. His job: to work with the White House and the Situation Room to determine the risk, what the response should be, and then how to assist the National Security Council.

One such decision involved a case familiar to many Americans, the Unabomber.

Ted Kaczynski, the so-called Unabomber, was responsible for a 17-year-long series of pipe-bombings that targeted business leaders, academics and others. The bombs, which were sent mainly by mail, started in the late 1970s before coming to an end in 1996. In all, the bombs killed three people and injured 23 others. His capture in Montana ended what was the FBI's longest and costliest manhunt.

Many experts believe it was Kaczynski's 35,000-word manifesto in which he called for an end to scientific research and a return by society to a simpler time that led to his downfall. A brother of Kaczynski's read the manifesto when it was published, and he alerted authorities. That tip eventually led to Kaczynski and his remote cabin. As agents prepared to raid that cabin, Worthington got a call.

"I was with the President in Hawaii. We were getting ready to do an activity. I figured it was to go play golf or take the girls, his daughters who were young at the time, to the aquarium there. But we got word through the Secret Service that something was going on. The

President needed to be on a phone call with the National Security Advisor and the National Security Council at the White House."

"We all know now what the outcome was (Kaczinski was captured without incident). But he (the President) was able to do the work because of something that our team had provided. The professionalism just takes over in situations like that."

Professionalism and mission success were the hallmarks of teams Worthington led in support of the Office of the President. While the job is stressful, Worthington said his teams were prepared for whatever challenge they might face.

"Everybody knew what to do. We were prepared for it. So, it wasn't like something that was out of the ordinary for us. Now, I don't mean to minimize the importance of what we were doing. But this was really just another day at the office. Whether it's calling a head of state or trying to get a hold of the astronauts in space or calling the latest football or baseball team that had just won a championship, it was something we did.

"It didn't matter what uniform you wore, whether it was one that was colored green, like mine, or whether you wore a blue or black suit like others, we all knew what we were there for. That made it much easier."

Even so, there are always situations and circumstances that can conspire to make things more difficult. Sometimes, they are deliberate. Other times, they are just situations that happen. That's when trust in your team becomes paramount.

"We were in Moscow and he (President Obama) was at a university, a business school there. It was just a beautiful location. But we didn't have the approved speech that he was going to give. President Obama really liked to use the teleprompter and he did very well with the teleprompter. So, we're waiting and waiting for the approved speech to come back from the White House where some last-minute changes were made. Literally, just before he walked on stage, we loaded the prompter with the new speech. We didn't have a chance to look it over and make sure it worked properly. We just trusted that everyone knew what they were doing."

It was during that same trip to Moscow, which was the first to the Russian Capital by President Obama, that Worthington found himself dealing with another challenging event. As with the previous speech at the business school, these prepared remarks and talking points also underwent a series of reviews by the White House. Since there must be an official record of all traffic, this communication was delivered by fax to a White House vehicle parked outside the Kremlin. That vehicle was affectionately known as Roadrunner.

"And so, we were sitting outside of the Kremlin and President Obama was about to go in and have a meeting with President Medvedev at the time. Colonel Michael Black (WHCA Director) was waiting with the senior staff and the Military Aide to the President inside the hallway just outside the meeting room. I was standing outside Roadrunner and kept getting repeated calls from our staff inside for the remarks. They needed them.

"Finally, the fax came. The operator handed it to me. I put it in my binder book. I ran up this long flight of stairs outside the Kremlin. There were several guards standing there. Now, we do wear a trip pin. The pin identifies you as part of the official travel party. Usually, you stop. They look at the pin and check your credentials. That time, I didn't give any of the Russians an opportunity to check anything. I ran up, I don't know, 100 stairs or whatever it was to the Kremlin. I handed the binder to the Military Aide, and it was handed to the President. He walked in the door. It was that quick. That was one of those things where as soon as it's done, you take that long breath, you put your hands on your knees."

THE NO-FAIL MISSION

The memories of his time at the White House are clear and vivid to Worthington. From the stories about Russia to the common days at Eighteen Acres, to even the ones that were top secret, one common thread remains, support for the Office of the President.

"I had some other jobs, but my responsibility was primarily for the President. There were only two times, though, when it was very secretive. It was the trips into the combat zones. Air Force One and the Office of the President are very big targets. They are strategic targets. So, when you go into a combat zone, you do take extra precautions. Whether it's the number of people you take, which is very small, or the fact that my wife did not know. In fact, nobody knew that I was flying out on two trips over into Afghanistan. I just didn't come home. My wife knew that if I didn't come home from work one day or she didn't hear from me, it was because I was on a trip where we couldn't talk about it.

"That can be challenging because the President's schedule is public. But for those visits to combat zones, they're always listed as nothing on the schedule, no scheduled activities, or a trip somewhere else."

It was during one such trip to Afghanistan where he and his team were waiting to take off from Bagram Airfield. It was just hours after President Obama had spoken to about two-thousand soldiers in a surprise visit.

Air Force One had left when Taliban militants fired at least one rocket at the base. It was a rare attack on a well-fortified base surrounded by mountains and desert. Worthington said it turned out the militants were aiming at his support plane. His flight was delayed until an all-clear was given to him and his team. While the Taliban claimed that the rockets hit a barracks, causing "heavy casualties,' a NATO spokesman says there were no casualties from the single rocket attack.

It was a little more than a decade later when Worthington retired from the Army (August 2021) after nearly 30 years of service to the country.

"I don't know that I ever thought, 'I love doing this because I'm serving my country doing this.' I did it because I was serving the office, and I was serving those around me who counted on me. Just like in combat, you don't do it for apple pie, mom and the flag. You take care of those around you. Certainly, I am proud to have served our nation, especially a nation at war. I still get goosebumps when I hear the National Anthem, see flags flying from cars and buildings. But what we do, we don't do for glory, for self-gratification or acknowledgement. We do it because love and live to serve others.

"I had the ability to serve someone whose greatest importance was that they serve the nation. I don't know that we who have done it think of it as such a huge thing, I think humility highlights our service. You are serving and protecting the men and women right around you."

That call to service is something that echoes through Worthington's words. But there are those lighter moments as well that become touchstones into a world that others can only imagine.

"There's a personal montage in my head of things we've done, things we've laughed at. I remember being laughed at in Russia for arguing over something and finding out that ten-thousand rubles was really only 50 cents. Or when my translator who was going back and forth with me and the Russian Communications representative assigned to help support me. I figured he was more than that, but Sergei made sure that I had whatever I needed for the visit. After all the back and forth, for an hour or so with my interpreter, Marine Sergeant Tim Serin, began speaking to me in Russian and to Sergei in English. I then decided to draw some pictures because of our mutual frustration with our inability to explain what I needed and that solved the problem.

The least technical solution to a problem—a kindergartner drawing—was the communications plan for the President in Russia. I have to laugh at that one."

"So, there are a lot of those things. When you are the Presidential Comms officer, you're the one standing on the side of Air Force One with a big cable in your hand. You have to run out to the plane and plug it in so that there can be official record traffic. Well, they can't shut the plane down until they know that they can fax something in and out. So, the first time you see that box is the first time you have EVER seen the box. That was a bit daunting when you consider you rehearse everything to perfection. But 'plugging the plane,' as we called it, was one of those crucible events for every Communications Officer in the White House.

"But on the flip side, that comms officer is the last person preventing that plane from taking off. I remember at Davis Monthan Airfield in Arizona; I unplugged the plane. I couldn't figure out how to get the door latched. In my head, what I was seeing was a big red flashing light in the cockpit saying, 'You're not secure. You can't take off. Not secured.' So, that was probably the most stressful moment for me. I thought I was the one who was going to be preventing the President from taking off and flying to the next site. That's pretty funny now when I think about it, but it was high stress for me."

Despite the stress and the challenges, Worthington is just one of many who say if the White House called again, they would answer and do so without hesitation.

"Absolutely. In a heartbeat. I loved it.

"There is so much that goes on to support the greater White House, which to me is also the Office of the President, the Office of the Vice President and the First lady staff. They're all in there. But there is just so much, it's amazing. Everything that has to happen to make that work. It's a very intricate dance, almost chaotic at times, that all comes together. It's really neat and interesting to see what work. All the things that are out there to support how the government runs and the government functions. I never would have had an opportunity (without this). I tell people that I got to see the other side of government, not the DOD federal government. I got to see the political side of the federal government. It was very eye-opening and very rewarding to me to see how the nation runs. And to be exposed to it. To have the honor to be exposed to that while in uniform. I'm a soldier, but I'm getting to see the politics of running a country. That was just an amazing experience, just being exposed to that."

Worthington served at the White House for a little more than two years, the last six months of President George W. Bush's term and the first year and a half or so of President Barack Obama's term. He said his last day was a bit melancholy as he realized this grand adventure was coming to an end.

"It was different. You have to turn in your black passport, your diplomatic passport. You want to have it back, but you can't have it back. There are so many cool stamps in it that you want to keep. You have to also turn in your trip pin. I still have my credentials, but they have a hole stamped in them so you can't use them again.

"It's not like you're losing your identity, but you almost feel like you're losing the ability to know everything that's going on. And that's it. It was an awesome experience.

"I remember afterwards my wife and I were watching TV and there was a trip somewhere or something was going on. I told her I know 'so and so's backstage doing this right now.' They've been there for a week. They have this. I wonder what hotel they're at. It was probably a year or two, where I was not depressed, but I would stare at the TV when on visits, knowing what was going on and wishing that I could still be a part of it."

For Worthington, nothing is more important than family, be it his White House family, his military family, or his own family. Service has been a hallmark of the Worthington family dating back decades. As he watches his sons grow up, he is hopeful that service will be front and center in their lives.

"It (service) comes in many different shapes and sizes and flavors. Being part of something other than just taking care of you is more rewarding. I do believe that many people, especially this younger generation, do want to serve. I just hope it's the right service. I believe though, and it's just a personal feeling, that everybody should do something to give back to their nation or to others. I think you learn a lot from doing that, before you take care of yourself.

"I will also tell people that it doesn't matter where you're from or what you've done. My dad went to school to be a seminarian. He went to seminary to be a preacher. We moved from Ohio to Texas. So, he got into seminary school. We were very lower middle class. I almost failed out of college. Now, I'm the one handing the phone to the President. Me. So, it doesn't matter where you came from. The military, at least from my perspective, the military portion of support to the President, you have the ability and opportunity to do anything you want. The people I worked with came from everywhere.

In his retirement speech, Colonel Worthington noted just how big an impact the military made on his life.

"The Army saved me. I was failing my way out of Syracuse University, spending too much time at the fraternity house and very little time in class. I was alone, lost and did not know what I wanted out of life. It was only because of a friend, Starr Moore, that I even decided to walk into the ROTC office one day… and I was hooked. I don't know what it was. I can't recall what it did to me other than providing me with a sense of purpose and direction, surrounded by a group of people who part of something larger than them.

"A few years later, as I took my oath of commission to, among other things, protect and defend the Constitution of the United States, I set my goals; 20 years, having done something good for someone, LTC and still have my family. Well, 30 years later, I feel confident I met my goals.

"But it was certainly not without setbacks, missteps and mistakes, a lot of mistakes. In fact, I would argue that the scars we carry around with us only make us better soldiers, better leaders, better people because they serve as a reminder of what was wrong—or what did not work.

"In fact, by all rights, I should not even be here today. I had to get a waiver for my eyesight just to stay in ROTC and then had to fight a medical board just ten weeks into my Infantry Basic Course—and I have held onto that medical board determination just in case I ever had to use it again.

"I have had the opportunity to do some incredible things, some really cool things. Whether it is jumping from airplanes and having to pull—and pack my own chute, serving in the Demilitarized Zone in Korea, flying combat missions in Iraq and Afghanistan with the best helicopter pilots in the world, working in the White House, flying on Air Force One, almost getting arrested in Moscow, walking the Great Wall of China, driving all over Europe with two of my favorite people—Lani Lemenger and Greg Rowland, driving cloud adoption and data standardization in our Army or leading Servicemembers in combat, I have amassed a lot of great memories of things I have done, seen or been a part of.

"But all of that pales in comparison to the people I have served and those who have impacted me. THAT is why we wear the rank we do. THAT is why we are unable to be at home when our families need us. The men and women I have worked alongside and the impact they have made on me—or that I have made on them—is what is truly important—not what I have done.

"I am so proud to be a soldier. Proud to be a member of a team of professionals where everyone can succeed, regardless of their background, upbringing, social status, race, or sex. We are all brothers and sisters, sons and daughters living the Army values as best we can, stumbling at times, and being there for each other in times of need."

Colonel Worthington also offered his advice to the leaders of today and of tomorrow. He said true leaders hold back the urge to provide the answer to every problem.

"By asking the right questions and using your influence and authority to enable them, everyone succeeds. Many times, our teams don't want to be told how to do things. They want to be set loose on the problem knowing they have your support."

And in many cases, Worthington said it comes down to the words you use. He referred to a phrase he heard from one of his favorite book and television series, Game of Thrones. "Words are Wind."

"That statement rings true for all of us. If you say something, mean it. If during your engagements, you tell someone you will "look into it" or "make it happen" then follow through. All too often, we encounter those who speak with hollow words because nothing ever happens, and they were just going through the motions. Prove them wrong—make it happen for them and do what you say. And if you cannot, tell them that—they will respect you even more for your honesty and transparency."

His career is a reminder that the team is stronger than the individual. During that retirement speech, he recalled a headstrong sailor who called him out for preaching teamwork, but not exhibiting it on road marches. Worthington learned from that experience. Instead of running most of the way and encouraging people to try to beat him, he tried something different the next time. He finished the march in the allotted time and because everyone walked with him, everyone passed. It was a lesson to him about how stronger we are together.

"I am so proud that our nation's military is made up of people from all walks of life, social backgrounds, ethnicities, and religions. It is what makes us strong. We are all united under one common cause and a bond of brotherhood that I don't know exists anywhere else than, possibly, law enforcement or first responders.

"That's one of the things that I've taken out of this. If I could do it, anybody could do it. All you have to do is try."

CHAPTER 6

I grew up on G.I. Joe

Roy Flores, Presidential Service Badge #27450

President Barack Obama poses for a photograph with Roy Flores at the White House Oval Office, (Photo courtesy: Roy Flores)

THE NO-FAIL MISSION

"Never in a million years did I think I would be at the White House. I was a latchkey kid. I grew up in The Bronx, New York City. My parents were first generation Americans that sometimes had three jobs. I had to be self-sufficient growing up."

For SFC Roy Flores (Presidential Service Badge #27450), his youth was built around the military. His father served, but his "touchstone" so to speak, was G.I. Joe.

"I grew up on G.I. Joe and other cartoons," he said. "It had every branch, the best of the best, put together for one cause."

At the time, G.I. Joe showcased the adventures of a "real American hero." Nearly 100 episodes of the cartoon aired in the 80's, providing tie-ins to both the comics and the toy line, which were quite popular at the time. In fact, sales of G.I. Joe and other so-called "war toys" rose more than 300 percent between 1982 and 1985, a time of relative peace in the United States.

Those toys and their creators also benefitted from a relaxing of standards involving children's programming, standards that many in the government and in the White House felt were too stringent. The pendulum swung back and forth in those years. It was a loud and boisterous debate that was lost on a young boy on the other side of the television screen in The Bronx. Even so, G.I. Joe was a foundational part for a boy who grew up in a military family. He could see himself being that action figure that helped to keep the peace around the globe. It was a feeling that was reinforced in his family structure, even if it was rarely discussed.

"My dad served in Korea. He never talked about his time in the Army. I never thought I would get to that level other than to see movies and read history books. I never thought I would get an opportunity to show my skill set and be honored to be a part of that."

Despite the role and the history of the military had in the Flores family, when Roy decided he wanted to be part of the military culture, it wasn't a popular decision within his family.

"My dad wasn't happy with my choice of joining the military at 17. I did two years of JROTC (Junior Reserve Officer Training Corps) in high school. He wasn't happy about that either. But at the end of the day, he just let me go."

"When he passed away (less than a year into my enlistment), some of his brothers came down and some of them were talking about how he never opened up. It's probably because he lost a lot of friends and saw some things. He got drafted. He knew the reality of what could happen. Maybe, that's why he didn't talk about it. He wanted to protect me."

"I see both sides. But I want to talk with people and share my experience. I've done everything from war zones to the White House, so I understood how he felt, especially now having kids of my own."

The Army life took Flores all over the world. In his 23 years of service, he spent more than half of that overseas. He spent the first part of his career in Germany working with Air Defense Units and Signal Units. He later was with the 18th Airborne Corps at Fort Bragg when terrorists struck on September 11th.

"I was with them for about four or five years and was part of the invasion of Iraq. My first tour was 13 months and then about three or four months later, I went back for another nine-month tour. When I came back, I was sent to Korea. I went to Fort Lewis after that, part of the Stryker Brigade. That's when I applied for and received orders for the White House."

The process wasn't as easy as it sounds. Flores found out about the role while stationed at Fort Lewis in Washington State. The interview process was unlike anything he had ever done before. He was in a room with one of the intelligence officers. Flores didn't know it at the time because everyone was wearing civilian clothes.

"It was interesting, because it was sort of a pressure test to see how you would respond and react. Well, I'm always going to be myself. It was a lot of digging through what you've done, where you've been, your credibility, your skill set, your experience.

"Seeing how you handle yourself was another thing too. Two doors down, I had a peer. He had a similar skill set. He didn't do too well because his ego got to him. Someone was asking questions and he got hot. He got personal about it. We could all hear him. It was interesting being able to have my conversation and then two doors down, hearing the conversation of good cop/bad cop.

"So, yea, it was definitely an experience. Once I got selected, it was ironic. I was in the Stryker Brigade at Fort Lewis, and I was told, 'You got selected, you're in. Congratulations.' I was still waiting for my orders when the same White House officials came back to Fort Lewis. They saw me and said, 'Hey, you know, you're supposed to be getting ready to go in like sixty days?' I said, 'No, I never received my orders.'

He said, 'Where's your unit? I'll take care of it.'

"A Sergeant-Major (SGM) at Fort Lewis had apparently misplaced them. But when I came in the next day, I had my orders. I was on the way to the White House. It was pretty powerful."

Flores was anxious, but he felt he was prepared for the new challenge. He credited the resilience he learned growing up, but also honed by the leaders who shaped him within the Army.

"I had some seasoned old school officers coming up. I came up in '94, so I still had some Vietnam era, you know, veterans and their mentality were different. Far more aggressive. The live or die mentality with everything you do. Just get it done. You don't get paid by the hour. You get paid by the quality and by the results. So, that kind of just stuck with me. So, it just evolved with the right people on the right missions. Just having that resilience here, that I always had as a kid, just never give up and move forward. That helped me tremendously."

That need to be nimble was never more necessary than in his role in support of the Office of the President. During his tenure, Flores supported more than 600 travel operations of the President, Vice-President, and First Lady. Those trips were both domestic and foreign.

"I've seen people go into panic attacks on trips and it's like, okay, what do we need to do? And how are we going to fix it? And then they come back around. Everyone is different, not just in the military, but in life."

Flores served as a J4, Assistant Service Material Division NCOIC, Warehouse NCOIC, Material Management NCOIC: WHCA and Certified as Operations NCO (OPSNCO) and Audio-Visual Technician (AVT). Those are a lot of letters, but in essence, he traveled in global support for operations for the President of the United States.

"(In this role), you're looking at the greatest country in the world and the most powerful person in the world. If something does go wrong, it's a huge embarrassment. And it ripples. It's a part of history. So yeah, it's totally zero failure. It's not like when you have different conflicts and battles, things can go on. If you fail at this, it's forever."

Flores faced several high-pressure situations during his time at the White House, where the outcome was far from certain. Even so, he said the chaos and high pressure brought out the best in him.

"Sometimes, it came down to using my skill sets from my past units, such as the 18th Airborne and just changing that and transferring it to a different environment. In those environments, it's also zero failure, but those failures aren't always noticed by the world.

"I always told my team that we have a plan. We know how to execute it. I told them not to be overwhelmed by the moment. I had a good team and sometimes we just had to sit down and talk about it.

"You don't always have time to build that independent trust or faith. You must have faith and trust in the uniform. That can be shocking to some people. It's also funny because I remember talking to some of my colleagues at the time. Some of them were talking about where they came from. I told them, it's not important. It's where we are right now. We all come from different units or missions, but right now, all we have to focus on is this. This is the Super Bowl. We don't have time to talk about the other pee-wee league matches we had. It's 'what do we have to do now?' So, it could be a shock to some people. You always had to be ready to execute.

"You're there because they're there. I remember running a trip when people were complaining about the rooms. I was like, 'Look, I don't care about your room, you're going to bunk up with somebody if you have to. We're here for the (POTUS) President and the (FLOTUS) First Lady and everyone else.'

"I'm not here to make sure you have a nice room by yourself, regardless of your rank. This is what we have. So, you do have some things like that, but overall, I'd say 99.9 percent of the people know the cause. When you have this camaraderie and you know that as a core, they will get things done. But yeah, there are always people who surprise me. I'm like we're not here to travel and see the sights. We're here to set up a mobile White House.

"It's not really that hard if you're calm and cool-headed and most importantly, if you have a good team. That doesn't mean you don't have Murphys (challenges). You can plan for contingencies, and we did, but there are always one or two that come through that you don't anticipate."

In a phrase, Flores called it always being "Semper-Gumby," meaning flexible. That flexibility was key for Flores and his team on a trip to Brazil. He had to commandeer a forklift to get things done. He said it was a matter of asking for forgiveness, not permission.

"There was a lot of brass and staff who didn't know who I was. I was in khakis and a buttoned shirt. I had been listening to them flip out for about five minutes. So, I jumped in and told them, 'This is who I am, this is who I work for (the President) and this is why I'm doing it.' I did it in a nice way, of course. I took the forklift and began loading the assets that needed to be loaded. I told them, 'I'm not here to wait for you.' I made the call, and later on, they said, 'Oh, okay. All right.'"

It was on a trip to Portugal that Flores took time out from his duties to recognize someone for a simple act of kindness. During the visit, the President remarked that after drinking some coffee that it was some of the best that he had ever had. Flores took it upon himself to find out where it came from.

"I felt like I had to find the guy. I always believe we should recognize people for what they've done. It meant a lot to me, because I believe that even a simple cup of coffee can mean something. When I found him and gave him a certificate thanking him, he was very, very proud and emotional. To see the excitement in his eyes, that personal touch is something that will be remembered long after we're gone."

Those "random acts of kindness" seem to be in short supply these days. However, when Flores left the military for the corporate world, it was something he carried with him.

"I believe gratitude is everything. Gratitude is the right attitude. Be thankful and recognize people. I guess it comes down to moral fiber and not being lazy. It only takes a second to say thank you, with a genuine handshake. Typing a certificate doesn't take long. I always made it a point to write down the names of people who went above and beyond."

It's also finding solutions amid the chaos that Flores remembers. He was overseeing a Presidential trip to Portugal when at the last minute, the wrong piece of equipment got to the wrong location and the President was left without the right podium.

"People were panicked. It was a speech outside and it wasn't the right podium. So instead of arguing about it, I'm like, 'where is it?' I grabbed a rental and talked to the police and let them know what we have to do here. We got it set up and we moved on. So, it was pretty funny, but I was just like, 'what do you need done?' People were so caught up in failing instead of executing."

After he left the White House, Flores received orders to Fort Drum, New York. That led to an eventual deployment to Afghanistan. It was roughly a year after he left the White House that he came face to face with his former colleagues, half a world away.

"It was the time that Brad Paisley came with President Obama (May 2014). Everybody was talking about a possible withdrawal at the time. Paisley had a concert and he spoke to a lot of soldiers.

"During that time, out of blue, one of the staff recognized me. Out of the thousands of soldiers there, they recognized me and my uniform. They offered to get me behind the ropes. I declined because I didn't want to leave the rest of my team behind, but it was nice to know that people still remember. That you can still have the bond and the high five and the hugs and catch up. It was cool. But there were also a lot of eyes on me, like 'who are you? What have you done?' A lot of the soldiers and leaders didn't know what I had done before. Other than when they saw my uniform, they saw a badge. So, there was just like, 'How do you know them? What have you done before?'"

Even now, the desire for service to others is still a huge part of Flores' life. He works to give back to a culture that's given him so much.

"I enjoy helping veterans. I just can't turn it off. I always tell them if I could take my cape off and still be Superman, you can do it too. I try to use that imagery. Clark Kent is Superman and Superman is Clark Kent.

"I do a program called 'Merging Vets and Players' on Fridays. It's designed to help combat veterans and athletes who are transitioning into their new uniform and their new life. So, I do a lot of listening and helping. Even some tough love when they need it. I always tell people I was in the Army, but I'm not the Army."

Flores is just one of several Presidential Service Badge recipients who have said if the White House called again, they would come running. But Flores also tempered that excitement with where he is in his life.

"You know, right now, I would. I would say I would be honored. But at the same time, the level of travel and having a family and being away from home and away from my two daughters, your mindset is a little different. But, never say never, you know. It was a great adventure."

His time at the White House was also history-making. Flores was there from 2009-to-2013, President Barack Obama's first term. It was at a point in history where the world was getting used to the first American President who didn't look at all like his predecessors. That was something not lost on Flores and his service to the Office of the President.

"I think it was more than the office at the time. During that presidency, it was more than the office. It was a person whose presence was something historic and different. It filled a lot of people with pride.

When I was a kid, around five or six, I loved history. I have always loved history. I asked my mother, 'why do all the Presidents look the same?' She told me that eventually there will be faces that will be different. It's just a matter of time. And it happened. The only sadness that I have is that my mother wasn't able to see that.

"It was an honor to support the greatest cause of leadership in the world. It was a privilege to be around these people from all branches who worked together to make sure the President had the ability to communicate and execute his goals for the world.

"I'd like to believe that we still have the Captain America spirit of caring and knowing that we have to take care of both the country and its citizens. 2020 showed me that everyone has an opinion. I explain to my kids, 'look you are going to see a lot of things, but I'm going to do what I think is right. You can't go wrong if you do what is right."

CHAPTER 7

Tomorrow can be a Better Day

Hervy "James" Oxendine, Presidential Service Badge #20138

President George W. Bush poses for a photograph with Hervy "James" Oxendine at the White House Oval Office. (Photo courtesy: Hervy "James" Oxendine)

THE NO-FAIL MISSION

The fall of 2003 was one of the worst firefighting seasons on record for Southern California. Spurred by the powerful Santa Ana winds, flames devoured thousands of acres of land, caused millions of dollars in property damage and worst of all, took more than a dozen lives. Air travel in and around the region was disrupted. Places that normally played host to sporting events, such as Qualcomm Field, home of the NFL's then-San Diego Chargers, were pressed into service as evacuation shelters. At one point, the fire was burning more than six-thousand acres an hour.

The response relied on cooperation and coordination between local, state, and federal authorities. The National Guard was mobilized, and President George W. Bush declared several counties in the region disaster areas, making them eligible for federal aid. As the fire reached containment, President Bush and his staff decided they wanted to be on the ground to personally thank those men and women who helped to prevent an even wider disaster. Once the decision was made to go, Hervy "James" Oxendine (Presidential Service Badge # 20138) and his colleagues sprang into action.

"Normally, on a stateside trip, you fly out to the trip site a week or two early to prepare for the President, Staff and Press Pool arrival. That gives you time to get your team there and get all your equipment on site. Arriving early also gives you time to coordinate services with the Secret Service, Press, and local authorities to coordinate functions and events prior to the President's, First Lady's and, or, Vice President's arrival. There are several important events you must plan for prior to their arrival: When and Where Air Force One will be arriving. What airport. What runway. And what time. You also need to know the route the President will take to and from the airport to the events, and the number and types of vehicles in the convoy. You must make sure that there are eyes on the President every step of the way. It can't be 99.99 percent, it has to be 100 percent, 100 percent of the time."

For the man affectionately known as "Ox," it was a chance to make a difference, an opportunity that he had been searching for his entire life.

His story begins in the rural areas of North Carolina, more specifically Robeson County, the home of the Lumbee Tribe of North Carolina. Oxendine grew up in Pembroke—a small community about 90 miles from the Atlantic and just a stone's throw from the South Carolina border. It was a poor area, generally speaking, with the median household income a little more than $18,000 a year based on figures from the 2010 Census. It was also the cultural and spiritual center of the Lumbee Tribe to which his family belonged. The Lumbee Nation was the largest tribe of Native Americans recognized within the state of North Carolina.

"I grew up just like any other kid in the South," Oxendine recalled. "I had a great family that loved me, fed me Southern food, and taught me how to live the Southern way. We weren't very political, but we were extremely spiritual. We were Southern Baptist. Politics was something we really didn't discuss in our house. Really, we didn't talk about anything related to the President, Vice President, or First Lady. I mean, growing up, I don't remember a single instance of when they (my parents) really talked about these topics."

In the early 1990s, Oxendine moved to live with his aunt in Monroe, North Carolina. It was here he attended and graduated from high school. He played high school and by his own admission, he just did the "typical stuff" and hung out with his friends. After a brief conversation with one of those friends, Oxendine decided to follow him into a Navy recruiter's office in Charlotte, North Carolina, a decision that would determine the course of his life.

"I thought to myself afterwards that I must have had a sign posted on my forehead that read, 'this guy doesn't have any clue about what he wants to do with his life.' The recruiters were salivating quite a bit when I introduced myself to them. I remember quite vividly one of them approaching me and asking quite bluntly:

'What are you doing after high school?'

"I remember telling them that I did some acting in high school, but my true interest was in art and graphic design. My tentative plan was to attend the Atlanta School of the Arts, but only after getting my act together and actually applying to the school. I believe the recruiters saw right through those empty words and began the process of recruiting me into the United States Navy.

"Years later, I would reflect on those decisions and discussions and admit to myself that this was truly the best decision for me at the time. It probably saved my life.

"I remember the recruiter quite well. In any other life, I would have thought he was a car salesman. He was extremely good at what he did. He was able to 'sell' the goodness of the Navy.

"The recruiter told me, 'We have some fantastic opportunities for you in the military. Some of the jobs will give you the ability to travel the world and visit exotic places. You will meet and work with some great people and do amazing work for your country.' They were the typical talking points that recruiters utilize to lure in and attract young people searching for adventures in faraway countries.

"To sweeten the pot, the recruiter offered me three separate locations for boot camp. He said I could go to Great Lakes (Chicago, Illinois), to Orlando, Florida or I could do to sunny San Diego, California. I immediately jumped on sunny San Diego because it was the furthest place from Monroe, North Carolina.

"To be honest, I hadn't really put too much thought or effort into joining the military. Other than my uncle who served in Vietnam, my family stayed away from military life. I think, maybe, my grandfather on my mother's side may have served for a short period of time, but I can't be sure. All I have is a photo of him and another guy with a Hawaiian girl in a tropical setting.

"That said, with being Native American, I learned at an early age that our people have served in every major military conflict for more than 200 years. Coming from a warrior society, the need and desire to serve my country had always been there. It just took the act of following a close friend into the Navy recruiters' office to make that happen.

"I remember spending my childhood running through the woods around my house, always building tree houses, forts, and barracks. We played soldiers and marines. We were all brave warriors fighting countless battles with my younger cousins and relatives.

"I vaguely remember watching countless military aircraft fly over my house and could even see the wheels and engines on the C5 and, or, C-17s, because of their weight, they also strained to gain altitude after taking off from Fort Bragg Army, even though Bragg was more than 40 miles away, the planes also seemed to be just reaching the tops of the tree lines at my house because of weight while they attempted to gain altitude, which scared the bejesus out me. I always said to myself, 'never me, never will I join the Army and find myself in those aircraft struggling to fly.'

"I found out many years later after growing up that most of those aircraft, if not all of them, were not actually coming from Fort Bragg. They were coming from Pope Air Force Base, which is collocated with Fort Bragg. I felt awfully silly when I learned that, but hey, what can you do, I was just a kid!"

Oxendine eventually made his way to boot camp in San Diego. It was July of 1993. And it was hot.

"I wasn't in the best of shape, and I didn't come to boot camp with the right mentality. I wish someone would have coached me and said, 'Hey listen, you are going to boot camp in San Diego. It's going to be for eight weeks. You're going to have to train. You're going to have to exercise. And you need to follow directions very carefully.' But nobody did.

"Now, one of the benefits of being in San Diego is that the Navy SEALs train over in Coronado. They're right next door to us. They always had an open invitation to come over to boot camp and 'cheer' up the recruits.

"If you didn't follow directions or other things, you got a free opportunity to exercise with the Navy SEALs after working hours and enjoy their Physical Training (PT) program with them and other recruits for about an hour or so.

"Navy SEALs have a true passion and love for what they do. They're not shy or skittish about sharing that love with anyone that may need some additional motivation. I fortunately got the chance to participate in some of these extracurricular activities on a couple of occasions at boot camp. It sure did motivate me to pay attention and always do the right thing.

"I successfully completed boot camp at the end of August 1993 and went on to spend the next two months at Navy Training Center (NTC) San Diego, learning how to be a 'radio man.'"

From San Diego, Oxendine received his first set of official orders. He scored fairly high in "Radioman A" school, which taught him the ins and outs of using voice and data circuits to keep communication flowing between units and between various groups involved in missions. His scores gave him the opportunity to go anywhere in the world. He chose NASKEF, the Naval Air Station at Keflavik, Iceland. The facility was located on the southwestern part of the island. It had a storied history. Built by the Army during World War II, it helped to not only secure critical air routes in the North Atlantic, but it also helped to deliver supplies and personnel to the European theatre. For Oxendine, it was another example of him "not following the traditional path."

After completing his tour in Iceland, Oxendine negotiated a set of orders aboard to USS Moosbrugger (DD 980), a Spruance-class destroyer built for the United States Navy by the Ingalls Shipbuilding Division of Litton Industries at Pascagoula, Mississippi. Affectionately nicknamed the "Moose" by her crews, she was named in honor of Vice Admiral Frederick Moosbrugger who is best known for his service in World War II as a highly successful commander of destroyer squadrons.

He successfully completed one deployment aboard the Moosbrugger, which was a four-month South American deployment called a UNITAS. A UNITAS is composed of sea exercises and in-port training involving several countries in North, South and Central America, conducted by the United States since 1959 in support of U.S. policy. After stepping off the ship in May of 1997, Oxendine reluctantly decided to separate from the United States Navy.

"At the time, I just knew this was something I did not want to do with the rest of my life. Fortunately, I had met my soon-to-be partner in April of 1997, while she was actively serving in the United States Navy at VP 30 in Jacksonville, Florida. We went on to have our first son in September of 1997. Between the stresses of not being able to find a decent paying job, taking care of a new family and having a tough but loving father-in-law who routinely encouraged me to take care of my family and rejoin the military, I finally found myself, after 18 months deciding to re-enlist in the United States Navy."

Oxendine had signed on for four years. He and his family found themselves in the United Kingdom. He reported to Joint Maritime Facility (JMF) St. Mawgan. The facility was nestled near a small farming community about four hours south of London. The command focused its mission on tracking and providing RF communication to ships and other surface vessels conducting operations in the local vicinity.

"Shortly after joining me in England, my wife and I enjoyed the arrival of our second son. He was born in Touro, United Kingdom. Life in England was great. Once you became accustomed to the weather and dreary days and nights, you learned to truly enjoy being there."

Oxendine and his family were in England during one of the darkest days in American history: September 11, 2001. Understandably, they were concerned, not just for their country, but for their friends and family who were there.

"I vividly remember the day. It was like any other day. I remember my team and my chain of command were standing in formation, preparing to receive the Plan of the Week (POW) from our leadership. I remember our Commander walking in with a somber look on her face, she did not smile while our team formed into ranks – after coming to attention, she softly and without hesitation informed us that two commercial airliners had just flown into the (two towers of the) World Trade Center. She was unsure if the incident was an accident or if it had been caused by terrorist attacks. As we turned on the TVs and began to watch the news, we saw the two towers were consumed in fire and smoke and the people below running for their lives.

"As the first building crashed down and the second building began to sway and shake, our hearts and our thoughts were with the people and their families who were involved in this devastating event. We then watched as the second building collapsed. The base went into lockdown. The building where we worked also went into lockdown. Our lives from that single point in time changed forever."

Three days later, on September 14th, President George W. Bush was at "Ground Zero." He gave his famous "bullhorn address" standing next to retired firefighter Bob Beckwith. The President called out to the first responders surrounded by wreckage as they mourned the loss of lives.

"I remember watching the President and how that whole scene played out. Of course, I was devastated about the whole incident. I felt horrible and sad for those directly affected by these attacks. Had I not already been in the military, I would have definitely joined that day, just like so many others did. I remember the bullhorn in his hand and the words he spoke to families, and to the world and to the terrorist who knocked those buildings down."

It was an anxious time not just for the nation, but for those entrusted with its protection. With uncertainty about who exactly was responsible and what the attack would mean, there was anxiousness around every corner. Multiple that by being overseas, and you have a recipe for a high-stress situation.

"It was a scary time for us too. Our facility was on lockdown. We had no idea where the attack came from, and we had no idea if they were going to target us because we were overseas."

It was then that Oxendine realized that he wanted to do more. He wanted to be more. And he continued searching for that elusive "something."

"You want to make your parents proud of you. You want to make them feel like you've accomplished something. So, when I saw that (the President at Ground Zero), something kind of clicked in my mind and I was like, somebody has got to be there. Somebody has got to be helping with the communication that gets him to that point."

Making sure that the President has what he needs to connect with a grieving world is something that stuck with Oxendine, even after the tragedy of 9/11 faded into his memory.

"A couple of years later, I came across an article in the Navy Times about the White House Communications Agency. I remembered my dad's words about making a difference and it all kind of just connected for me."

Oxendine started making phone calls to detailers, community managers, and even recruiters in hopes of finding a solid lead on how to apply to the WHCA.

"I spent the next several months doing research, making phone calls, and even looking for prior members of WHCA to talk to in order to learn how to apply for this prestigious program. I eventually started calling numbers within the White House and was able to find someone who had a contact within WHCA. He shared the number with me and that led me down the right path.

"Once again, I didn't take the traditional path. Eventually, I was able to get my foot in the door and speak directly with the Military Hiring manager within WHCA, who assisted me in applying for this program.

"After a lengthy wait, I was notified via message traffic that I had been selected to take orders to the White House Communications Agency. My commander at the time made it known that I had been hand selected to this prestigious program and that I would be working for the President of the United States. She loved those words, 'hand selected.'

"The first thing I wanted to do was tell every member of my family. My mom wanted to know if I was going there to protect the President. I said, 'No, I'm not Secret Service.' But in a way, though, I was protecting the President. I was giving him what he needed to do his job."

THE MEN AND WOMEN BEHIND THE PRESIDENTIAL SERVICE BADGE

To work for the President, Oxendine was required to obtain a "Yankee White" clearance. In Oxendine's case, the review took about six months. Investigators talked to relatives, neighbors, and associates. It was an exhaustive effort for everyone involved. Oxendine eventually received his security clearance and found himself in Washington.

"I remember the first time going to Building 399 on Anacostia Naval Base, which is the headquarters for the White House Communications Agency. More than 500 military, civilians, and contractors work within the building. Most of the equipment that is used by WHCA technicians is also in the building. I remember stepping through the gates at the guard shack and noticing how heavily armored the Marines were that occupied the front office and just thinking to myself this can't be real.

"I was just speechless. I mean, I didn't want to say I was just a poor kid from the South. But it was amazing that someone with my background and upbringing could actually make it to the point where they are working for the White House. It's almost impossible to describe."

Oxendine had no idea where he was going to work. Eventually, he met his sponsor and was told he would be placed in the 3PCC (3rd President Communication Command). 3PCC is responsible for providing worldwide communication support and services to the President, the Vice-President, the First Lady, Press and Staff of the United States. Being under the command of the 3PCC gave him the ability to travel both on state side missions and overseas missions. In those missions, his tasks including setting up communications for the president so he could address whatever audience he needed.

There were three teams assigned to the President and they each rotated weekly or monthly based on several factors, including location and duration of the trip as well as the needs of the Office of the President.

"Being assigned here was such a surreal feeling. Every day I was actually excited to show up to work. I never knew what to expect. I never knew where I would be going or who I would be around. The opportunities were only limited by your imagination and what you wanted to do. Even thinking about it today, it still feels unreal. It still feels like I imagined the whole thing.

"I remember one of the first shuttle trips I took down to Eighteen Acres (White House), dressed in a blue pinstriped business suit, with a tie and dress shoes on and I remember thinking to myself this can't be real. I don't really have access to the White House. As the barrier lowered and the shuttle pulled forward, we entered the driveway that gives cleared participants access to the front side of the White House. As I stepped off the shuttle, I looked up and the blue sky and then looked forward to the White House – amazed and excited. I followed the team into and through the guard house. Cleared to enter the White House, I stepped forward and walked toward The West Wing, still in amazement and grinning ear to ear as I walked toward the main command.

"I think about it now. It was almost impossible to think that I made it through the screening process. I was selected. Me. Somebody gave me a badge to walk into the White House. You really are hit by the magnitude of the access you are granted. The permission that you have to be in the room, to be around the President and his cabinet when decisions are being made. All that stuff is just so unreal. I don't think anyone can really fathom that.

"I remember my dad telling me a story about one of his first cousins and how he worked as an HMX-1 pilot for one of the Presidents in the late 60's, early 70's and how this great accomplishment brought honor and pride to his Native American community and family. The probability of these types of events occurring in our family are so rare that when they do occur, they are passed on from generation to generation, family to family and eventually turn into some type of folklore or myth as time passes by. Sometimes I wonder if my story and my journey will be passed along to the generations to come in hopes of sparking that same nontraditional path and journey spark in my relatives and family members."

There are two types of teams at WHCA, there are travel teams and there are fixed mission teams. Oxendine's orders called him to be on a travel team. His team had a very colorful moniker.

"We were called the "Black Sheep of the Command, which was a fitting name for our group. We were a ragtag bunch of service members, who worked hard and of course played twice as hard when we weren't on duty."

In October of 2003, "Ox" was given the opportunity to deploy on his very first Presidential mission to San Diego. The President was going to make a special trip out to California to speak to the firefighters, front line defenders, EMTs and other personnel battling the Cedar Fire. The blaze eventually burned more than 273-thousand acres (1,106 km2) before it was brought under control.

Oxendine was assigned to the campgrounds where all the firefighters, EMTs and all other fire/safety personnel were camping out as they fought the fire. He was given oversight of three large recreational vehicles (RVs), equipped with network and communication equipment to be utilized by the President, Secret Service and Press/Staff while visiting the campgrounds.

"We worked out a plan where the President would have the center RV. One would be for staff and the other would be a command station. So, if the President needed to rest or sit down between meeting with people, he would be able to do so."

Oxendine remained at the trailer compound as the day wore on. People had been coming and going throughout the event. It was then that he caught a glimpse of someone he had watched many times on the silver screen.

"So, we were hanging out and it was probably late in the afternoon and a crowd of people came by. The President is out somewhere, and this crowd shows up. In the middle is (California Governor-Elect) Arnold Schwarzenegger. And it's (California Governor) Gray Davis. They have their entourage around them.

"I had no clue if they had plans to come inside the RV or if they were just standing there on their way across the campground. I quickly grabbed my camera and headed outside of the RV.

"I knew this was my one and only chance to get a photo with me and Arnold Schwarzenegger. Having my WHCA lapel pin gave me the ability to quickly infiltrate this circle and get within an arm's reach of Arnold (Schwarzenegger). I could have stuck out my arm and patted him on the back shoulder. That probably wasn't the best idea, so I kept my arm to my side.

"He was a little shorter than I expected, but he was much broader than I ever suspected. Even so, I was still extremely excited to be that close to him. The crowd began to move forward with me still behind him and my intent was to find the perfect moment, where he's not talking and tap him on the shoulder and ask to take a picture with him, so I patiently waited for the exact moment, which never came – his security detailed asked him to hurry along, as they needed to get to get him to the "COPTER" to fly to one of the event sites.

"Devastated by this turn of events, I quickly departed the group and headed back to the RV to finish out my detail for the day. With that being said, I was stoked by the opportunity to be within arm's reach of the Terminator and live to tell the story about my encounter. That's the type of access that you would never get anywhere else."

Even today, more than a decade removed from his time at the White House, Oxendine remembers each situation and each colleague as if the events that brought them together were yesterday. It was a time in his life that he won't soon forget.

"I keep in close touch with a couple of the good friends that I had in the White House because the bonds are so strong. I think the kind of prestige that you get from working there and the friendships you develop there are partly because of the time you spend together, but they stay strong because there aren't very many people who could ever say, they worked in the White House. They traveled with the President. They spent time talking to the President. So those bonds, just like in the military, are very tight knit.

"I felt like we were the cream of the crop. I felt like these were some of the most intelligent people that I ever had the opportunity to work with in my career, in my life. Everyone was dedicated. It was one of those jobs that people enjoyed doing, no matter what. They wanted to be there. People weren't leaving at 1600 every day. They were happy to be there. The quality of life was good.

"Never in the rest of my military career did I ever come across a command where everybody just got along. It was probably the most professional organization. I know they screen these people hard. You had to have the right recommendations from the right people and of course, you had to go through all of the checks, including a financial background check. And even after you get there, nothing was taken for granted. You had to be professional.

"Usually when you put a ton of 'type A' personalities working together, it normally ends with those people at each other throats because there can be only one 'right way.' But that wasn't the case here. There was not one single instance, at least that I saw, where people got in trouble. That's because they respected their positions. They respected what they did. They knew they were just as talented as the people they were working with. So, it wasn't a real competition with lots of ego. Everybody was on the same level. Now, there were people of higher ranks, of course, but they easily shared whatever they knew. They cared. Everybody seemed to just care. I know that sounds crazy, because I've never been anywhere else in my career where the people just naturally cared and wanted to make sure the mission was done.

"I think the folks who were coming in, were kind of at the top of their game, both professionally and personally. There's symbolism with working in the White House, you know why you are here. You know that the work you are doing is both national and international in scope. So, I think everyone had the same singular belief, who we're doing this for and why we're doing it. I think is also helped that everyone seemed to be humble."

That humility is something that Oxendine witnessed first-hand, not just from his colleagues, but from the President himself.

"We did an event at Bolling Air Force Base (which later became Joint Base Anacostia-Bolling in Washington D.C.) with the President. I was standing off stage with him. You could tell that he was soaking wet. His coat, jacket, slacks, and shoes were all covered. Out of the blue, he just starts talking with me. I don't remember exactly what he said, but at that moment, I thought, 'He's just an average guy who's been given an extraordinary responsibility and now I'm just standing here with him, me a Lumbee kid from North Carolina, and we're talking about the rain.'"

In addition to spending time with the President, Oxendine also found himself face to face with Vice-President Dick Cheney, Secretary of State Condoleezza Rice, Defense Secretary Donald Rumsfeld, and Secretary of State Colin Powell.

"I was coming down in the elevator at the El Presidentia in Monterrey, Mexico. The elevator stopped and all of these guys got in, followed by an older couple. So, the big guys are surrounding this couple. And he starts talking to us wife. I remembered the voice. At first, I thought it was James Earl Jones, Darth Vader, right? But he turned to face me, and it was Colin Powell standing next to his wife. It was so special to be around those folks. There are so many of those types of encounters with staff and with reporters. Each one was special."

"I just, I feel lucky. I also feel privileged to know that my dad was around long enough to see that I worked there (and with them)."

Being able to think quickly on his feet and fighting through challenges were skills that Oxendine developed and honed during his time at the White House. He also quickly learned the amount of resources necessary to support the President of the United States, even for a relatively short visit.

It was during one such trip that Oxendine found himself near Busan, South Korea's second largest city and home to Fleet Activities Chinhae, operated by the United States Navy.

"We spent two and a half weeks there. This was part of an Asian trip that would take the President to several countries. So, there were a lot of people there. Secret Service, the White House, State Department. Lots of people were there. I remember standing on the tarmac from the moment that Air Force One landed to the moment Air Force One left. It wasn't long. The President just made a brief visit to the troops, maybe 30 minutes in length. But the President felt like it was important to be there and to show them that their mission is important, so we did it. I knew it meant the world to the airmen who stood there and listened to the President say, 'Listen, the work you're doing is important. You're important. I'm glad it was able to get here and see you guys and tell you personally, thank you for what you're doing.'"

THE NO-FAIL MISSION

While assigned to this mission, Oxendine was given the responsibility to "plug" Air Force One. That "plugging" allowed the Presidential plane, once landed, to have both phone and fax capabilities. After opening the box above the front tire on Air Force One and inserting the cable, Oxendine did an about-face and stood on the other side of the stairwell. The President used the stairwell to exit the plane and got into the Beast (the Presidential Limo), but not before first saluting Oxendine and others who were on the tarmac. Even before the plane arrived, the emotion of it all hit Oxendine.

"I remember standing on that tarmac waiting for Air Force One to arrive (at OSAN AFB). I listened through my earpiece to news that the plane would be landing in five minutes. I realized just how lucky I am. I thought about how my family from my small town and from my Native American Tribe would be so proud of me and the job I was doing for this country."

It wasn't just outside Air Force One where Oxendine found himself. He also spent time on the Presidential plane as well.

"I spent time in the President's office on Air Force One. I was putting in some video compression software to help the President communicate with anyone in the world easily. So, they wanted me to test it. I'm sitting in the President's Chair, looking out his window and testing this. I mean, how many people in the world can say they had an opportunity to do this. It was just so amazing. I felt so privileged. I mean, a young kid from North Carolina. My wife, we're both Native American, and this is by far one of the greatest things that I could have ever experienced in my career."

His heritage is clearly something that is central to Oxendine and his life. For the past several years, he and his wife have operated a non-profit that supports at-risk youth on the Pine Ridge Indian Reservation in Pine Ridge, South Dakota.

"So, the charity that (my wife and) I run dates back to 2002. I've had so much support before, during and after I was at the White House. All the way up my chain of command, it's been special. They've offered help, anything from going out to potentially supporting my work in South Dakota. It really was in its infancy when I was working at the White House and had it not been for the folks there, it might have died on the vine, but they were so supportive that it kind of grew and flourished from there. And two decades later, we're still doing it."

After the White House, Oxendine continued his military career. Afloat, he served aboard the USS Stockdale (DDG-106) and the USS Ronald Reagan (CVN-76). Ashore, he was assigned to NCTS Bahrain (Manama, Bahrain), NIOC San Diego (California), NMT Ford Mead (Maryland), 25/21 NCPT Fort Meade (Maryland) and COMTENTHFLT Fort Meade (Maryland). He dealt with Cybersecurity, Threat Intelligence and Threat/Risk Assessments. Quite a change from a young man growing up in North Carolina with no real plans for his future.

"It takes a lot of work, but the work is important. To the people who are reading this, I would say, every individual you read about is very humble. They know they are fortunate to be able to participate in something that contributed to the success of the country and often the world. These folks are all extremely humble and thankful for the opportunity. They value the gift they've been given to be able to do this. If given the opportunity I would go back in a heartbeat. The people, the mission and the symbolism are reason enough to go back and do the job and do the job well."

CHAPTER 8

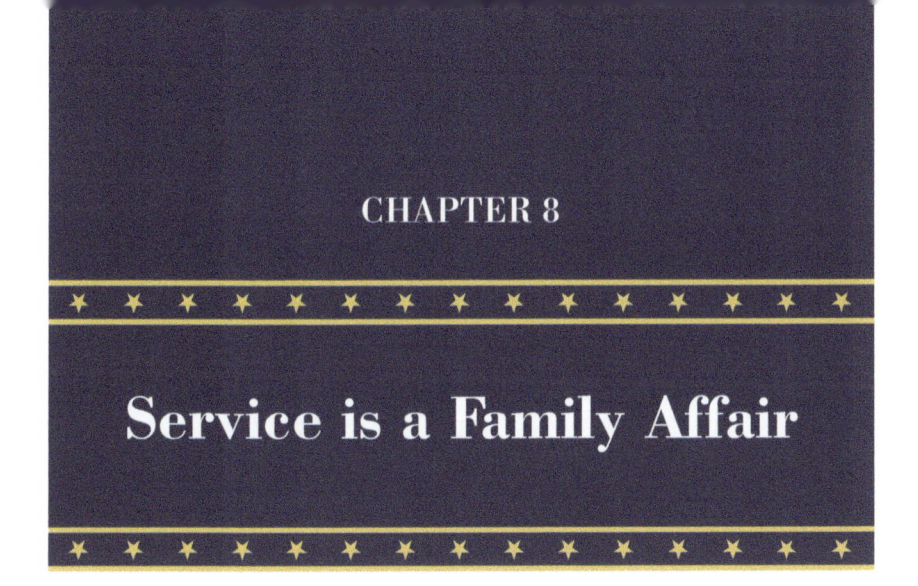

Service is a Family Affair

Scott Jones, Presidential Service Badge #19406

Scott Jones in front of the Presidential Limo at the funeral of Pope John Paul II, April 2005.
(Photo courtesy: Scott Jones)

THE NO-FAIL MISSION

April of 2005 brought leaders from around the world to Vatican City to pay tribute to the life and legacy of Pope John Paul II. It was one of the world's largest gatherings of leaders in history. In all, more than 100 countries were represented including 65 heads of government and ten separate sovereigns. In that crowd was President George W. Bush. Making sure he got there was Army Sergeant First Class Scott Jones (Presidential Service Badge #19406). Of course, in a role like this, getting there was half the battle.

"The President had made the decision that he did not want to fly the country's flag. He wanted to fly the Papal flag on the limo. So, we had a little bit of a run around trying to find a (Papal) flag. President Bush wanted to fly the (Papal) flag in honor of the Pope."

Jones served at the White House for more than six years after stints both home and abroad. In his role at the White House Transportation Agency, Jones was responsible for helping to coordinate all of the motorcades at home and abroad. He was also tasked with taking care of all of the staff luggage, including oversight of the search with the K-9 and Secret Service before it was loaded onto Air Force One.

The story of the White House Transportation Agency is as unique as the people who work there. Known colloquially as the White House Garage, it was created by an Act of Congress during the Taft Administration. At its founding in 1909, it consisted of one open "Pierce Arrow" touring car and five civilian coachmen. The transition to military chauffeurs began in the Hoover Administration, but it took until the Eisenhower Administration to complete. In September of 1963, the "White House Garage" was re-organized into a regular Army unit known as the U.S. Army Transportation Agency to serve in direct support of the President.

As part of his duties, Army Sergeant First Class Scott Jones was also part of the site survey teams that would go in advance of the President to map out travel routes. His teams also worked with embassy personnel on the ground to make sure the White House had everything it needed to make the visit a successful one.

It was quite a role for someone who, as a young boy from Eastern Pennsylvania, recognized that he needed a change in his life if he was going to live.

"Let's just say that I wasn't a good kid," Jones recalled. "I had friends. I just knew that the path I was on wasn't a good path. I was in a little town called Northampton. I was working at a place called Cross Country Clothes. I knew I just had to get away. There were too many things that were going on that weren't good. I knew I wasn't on the right path.

"One night I was lying in bed and thinking about it. And I said, 'you know what? I have to change my life.' I decided then I was going to go into the Army. I got up that next morning and went to the recruiter and said, 'I want to join the Army.' My friends didn't even know I was doing it. I just did it.

"It (joining the Army) scared me. It scared me a lot because I knew who I was. I was about to go on an adventure where I didn't know anybody. I knew my uncle had been in Vietnam, but other than him, I didn't know anybody who had been in the military. So, I was heading out on something that I knew nothing about. But I knew I had to do something to get away."

The decision to join the Army was not just a surprise to his friends, but to his parents as well.

"I remember my parents saying, 'You're not going to pass the test.' I have an older brother who tried to get in, but he didn't pass the test and he gave up. I said, 'Mom, I'm passing the test. I'm going to join the Army.'

"They were just like, 'Yeah, okay.'

"So, the day came, and I said to them, 'Hey, I need to move all of my stuff from my apartment into the house. The army recruiter is picking me up in a couple of days.' They were looking at me like, 'what?'

"I said, 'Yeah, I'm leaving and going in the Army. I told you I was going into the Army.' They said, 'okay.' They had a little party for me and moved all of my stuff into their house, up in their attic. A couple days later, I was gone."

Jones' first stop was basic training at Fort Dix, New Jersey. It was a challenging time, but he had convinced himself that he would make it through. Jones finished basic and went to his first duty station in Mannheim, Germany. From there it was back stateside to Massachusetts, then to the 305 Supply Company in South Korea. He later returned to Germany, first at Darmstadt and then to Heidelberg before being sent to Texas as a recruiter. Along the way, he got married to a girl back home.

"I knew (Lisa) before I even went in the Army. We were from the same town, and we had stayed in contact. When I was at my first duty station (Mannheim, Germany), I flew home, and we spent some time together. I asked her to marry me. Then, I went back to Mannheim. I eventually flew back, and we got married. She went with me to Fort Devens, Massachusetts. She wasn't my high school sweetheart, but she was and is my sweetheart."

To this day, Jones doesn't know how he landed on the radar of the people at the White House, but he was happy they came calling.

"I was serving as an Army recruiter in Texas. I really don't know how it happened. First, I got a letter saying they were interested in talking to me about coming to the White House to be a driver, and that somebody would be coming to Texas to interview me.

"Eventually, I got an email asking me to go to the Corpus Christi International Airport at a certain time on this day. Somebody would be there to meet me and talk to me about a position in the White House.

"So, I got to the airport. It was weird because I really didn't know where I was going. But when I walked through the front door, these guys were standing there. I guess they were TSA guys. They had a picture of me. They told me to come with them. They took me to a back room. I was like, 'oh, okay.' So, I went into this back room, and they put me there. There was a big table. There were a bunch of chairs. They closed the door and left. I was there all by myself.

"Then these two other guys walked in. They were kind of investigators. They told me to sit down, and they said, 'We'd like to talk to you about a position at the White House.' I was like, 'okay,' and they started to open up a folder. They pretty much had my whole life in that folder. They already knew everything about me. And then, they asked me if I was interested. I said, 'Yeah, I need to talk to my wife about it. But I'm interested.'

"Well, we've pretty much done everything on your background. We know everything. We've talked to your ex-girlfriends. We've talked to everybody. If you're interested, we already have you cleared to come to the White House.'

"They went so far back that they talked to people I didn't even know. I didn't remember their names. They went back to when I was a young teenager, 12, 13 years old. They went way back. It was then that I had people calling my parents asking if I was in trouble. They wanted to from them if I was going to jail. I don't know why they do it. But the investigators don't tell people why they're investigating somebody.

"I guess they wanted to see if I'm reliable, trustworthy, have anything against the government. I guess. When I told my folks that I was going to the White House, they were really happy. But they told me they wished they would have known when all this was going on. (The investigators) never talked to my parents. They talked to my neighbors, and I guess from them, they talked to old friends. But no, they never talked to my parents."

Jones and his wife Lisa relocated yet again, this time to the Washington DC area. Being from Pennsylvania, it was a welcome change as it got them closer to home and to family.

"I think it was good. I think she was happy to get back up this way. We were from Pennsylvania so going to DC would put us a lot closer to home. We had been away from home for a long time. Before we were in Texas, we had been living in Germany for eight years. So, she was pretty much glad to get back home and be closer to family that we could just go visit."

It took Jones a couple of weeks before he had his first "official" day at Eighteen Acres, but it was a time he would never forget.

"It was probably two or three weeks after I was at the White House Transportation Agency. We were at a building—we're not there anymore—but we were at a building on 22nd street. It was an older building that used to be a car dealer or something back in the day. It had elevators that took cars up and down the floors.

"Anyway, my first day was probably about two or three weeks after I'd been in the agency (that I went to the White House). I was just surprised that the little badge they give you. How much power that little blue badge really has. I mean we just walked right past the Secret Service, and right into the White House. When I was on the tour, they took me right into the Oval Office. We basically had free range (of the building). We just walked anywhere. I was like, 'wow, I'm just walking around the White House and nobody's even questioning me.'

"It was very weird. Because even though we would walk through metal detectors and have change or keys or whatever in our pocket and the detector would go off, we would just keep on walking. As long as we had that (blue) badge, we just walked right through."

Jones found himself in the heart of the Executive Branch, serving the Office of the President. During his entire Army career, he had not heard that such a posting was even available.

"I didn't even know they had that position (at the White House Transportation Agency) in the Army. I had no idea until they came to me. That was the first time I even heard of it.

"I can't speak for how it is now, but when I was there, we had a civilian guy in charge. He was a retired Sergeant Major from the Army. I think he was a GS-15. He was Director of the White House Transportation Agency. He told everybody when they got there, once you arrived there, then you could forget about ever going back to the 'real' Army. Once you got cleared for that 'Yankee White' security clearance, you weren't going anywhere. I got called a couple of times, but those people were told, 'we can't touch you. You're on special assignment.'

That "special assignment" took on many forms over the years. Initially, when Jones got to work, he spent the first two or three months learning his way around the District of Columbia. There were a number of different routes to learn as well as all the different streets. He was fast becoming a "local."

"When one first gets to the agency, you're only allowed in the car as a passenger. Eventually, they allow you to go out on a driving test. It's done by one of the senior people. Once you pass that test, you are actually allowed to go out there and start driving staff members on your own around the DC area.

"Once people get to know you, you move up. You can be out there traveling, taking part in motorcades there as well as motorcades in DC."

As Jones grew in his role, he eventually was tasked with taking care of the senior staff. That included trips back and forth to the Hill. He would pick them up at their residences in the morning and take them home at night. In addition, Jones and his team would handle all of the luggage for the senior staff on trips, both domestic and overseas. His group made sure they were also taken care of when it came to hotels, etc. He would also work with the Secret Service on routes and run them as needed.

"I don't think we ever had to adjust our routes. The Secret Service would pretty much give us two or three routes and on the night before we would get the primary route. We knew all three, but that was the one we would take."

During those duties, Jones never forgot his roots, nor the group that helped to get him there.

"Most of the staff, the senior staff and all of the people we used to drive around, they didn't know we were Army until we actually told them we were Army. They were kind of impressed that the Army was doing that and that we were here. They didn't know. They just thought we were government employees."

However, during these trips around the District, Jones got to know those senior leaders in government, and they got to know him. It led to some unusual encounters and some memorable relationships that he values to this day.

"I often picked up Karl Rove (Senior Policy Advisor and Deputy Chief of Staff to President George W. Bush). He was a comedian. Most passengers just sit in the backseat. He would refuse to do that. He would get in the front and the first thing he would do is grab the (radio) mic. He would call into our dispatcher. He would let the dispatcher know the route and wherever we were going. He would know all of the call signs, know exactly how to talk on the radio. Karl would also sit there and play with the lights and sirens. I would always have to 'yell' at him so that he wouldn't get me into trouble. But it was just our thing. He loved to have fun and joke around.

"I used to pick up Fran Townsend (Former Homeland Security Advisor to President George W. Bush) at her house all the time in the morning and took her home at night. We would talk and joke around a little bit.

"I also took care of Scooter Libby (Former Chief of Staff to Vice-President Dick Cheney and as well as Assistant to the President). Now, he had some problems."

Those "problems" were well-chronicled. I. Lewis "Scooter" Libby served from 2001 to October of 2005 when he was indicted on five counts, including perjury, obstruction of justice and making false statements, in connection with the Valerie Wilson case. That case involved the leak of the covert identity of the Central Intelligence Agency (CIA) officer. It was a major scandal for the Bush Administration and one that ensnared the highest-ranking White House official (Libby) since the Iran-Contra affair of the late 1980s. Libby was eventually sentenced to 30 months in prison. He appealed and when that process failed two years later, President Bush commuted the sentence, calling it excessive. However, the President did keep in place the conviction, the fine and the terms of probation. While Jones didn't talk about the case itself, he did bring up his encounters with the senior official.

I used to pick him (Libby) up at the Tidal Basin. Sometimes, he would jump in the backseat and say, 'Okay, I'm going to lay down here on the floor.' He would say to let him know when we're out of there. Once we got to a spot where nobody could see him, he would sit back up. When I took him to the White House, he would also lay down in the backseat so nobody could see him."

Jones served at the White House across both terms of the George W. Bush Administration. He was with the President countless times, both here and abroad, including time on Air Force One in such global hotspots as Pakistan.

"(One time) we were in Pakistan, and we were aboard Air Force One as we were landing. I guess we were probably about 30 miles out, when all of a sudden, the pilot informed us that everyone needed to close their blinds. He told us we were in territory that wasn't considered friendly. So, we shut our blinds and he shut off the lights and we went in under blackout. He used his night vision gear. They shut off all the runway lights too, so we went in under complete darkness. Everything was completely dark and that was kind of a little bit scary.

"They were watching the press corps pretty close because there were concerns that someone would mistakenly lift up the shade a little bit and let some light in, but they didn't touch anything."

That flight landed without incident. However, that was not the case in neighboring India where a similar trip could have landed them on the front page had it not been for some last-minute resourceful thinking from Jones and his team on the ground.

"Well, I don't know if it was the President, his aide, or his valet. I don't want to put the blame on any one of them. Someone left his briefing book on Air Force One. We had to go back and get it before everything started. And it was…it was pretty crazy. We didn't have much time to do it.

"We got lucky. The Secret Service talked with their counterparts in India who helped. Well, they got us back to the aircraft pretty quick. But then, coming back from the aircraft to the hotel. You know, there's a lot of traffic because of the motorcade and all the streets and everything being blocked off. And then you have all of the other traffic coming in. So, there was a big traffic jam. We were flying down the highway, probably doing about 70 miles per hour, two motorcycles in front of us, two motorcycle cops. We came up on a traffic jam just out of the blue, but there was an opening in one of the guard rails. So, the police turned and went right through the opening. We went straight into traffic. Everything was coming toward us.

"So, we were doing about 70 miles an hour with traffic coming straight at us and the cops were just waving cars out of the way. The person I was with, his name was Maldonado, Staff Sergeant Maldonado. He videotaped this on his phone because he thought he was going to die. He wanted his wife to see how this happened. Fortunately, we made it back and the President got everything he needed.

"It took a while to settle down because I was a mess. We were on the wrong side of the highway, and we were literally watching cars mash up into guardrails to get out of our way. It was really crazy."

While not all of those travels were as exciting as his journey to India, Jones did take several Presidential trips during his six-plus years at the White House.

"I don't know how many countries I traveled with President Bush. I've been all over the world.

"We went to China. We went to Russia. There was one time in Russia where we were supposed to pick up the luggage from Air Force One when it landed. We would take it to the hotel. I tried to get to the airfield in Russia. Everything was supposed to have been arranged with the Secret Service. Everything was supposed to be fine. But when the plane landed and I was supposed to go there, I was being held at gunpoint. They wouldn't let me go anywhere. I was being held by the Russian Army. They were just like, 'no, you can't go.' I was like, 'I have to go.' Well, you know, it is their country.

"There was another trip—and I don't remember the country. But when President Bush got on the plane (Air Force One), he turned around and asked if we had anybody left on the ground. He said, 'make sure we before we leave here, that all of our people are either on his plane or the other plane.' He made sure that we were all safe. We might have been stranded for a while if he hadn't."

That concern for others in his care was something that Jones noted on more than one occasion from President Bush. There were times when Jones drove the Bush daughters to Camp David. He also drove the President's brother, Florida Senator Jeb Bush, to the Presidential retreat on numerous occasions. Jones recognized the President as a family man and in terms of family, he remembered that the President also the importance of that in others.

"I used to have to go to Texas, to the President's ranch at Christmas time. They would go there every year, for about two weeks. I think it was my second year down there when the President asked me, 'You're married?'

"I said, 'Yes, sir.'

"He said, 'where's your wife?' The President told me that, 'From now on when you come down here, bring your wife.' So, she started coming to Crawford for Christmas."

There were also times shared by family at the White House, especially during the holidays. The Christmas season was a special one, but Lisa Jones recalled one summer holiday that was magical.

"It was the experience of a lifetime," she said. "We did the Fourth of July at the White House. That was really nice. We sat on the lawn. They had ice cream and hot dogs for everyone. We watched the fireworks, and the President came out on the balcony so we could all watch together. We did take our youngest son one Fourth of July. It was really nice. It was like family."

Jones also noted one event in which the President made fun of himself.

"I don't remember where we were flying but before the trip the President had been eating a little bag of pretzels and he choked on them. He choked pretty bad actually. But after it was all over, a couple of people razzed him. He would joke with people too. So, the word got out and when we got on the aircraft, everybody had a bag of pretzels on their seat. He made sure everybody got a bag of pretzels. I know everybody knows he was looked at as a serious personality and everything like that. But when he wasn't around all the press, he would talk to you, man to man, and joke with you."

There were also other times when the President "gave as good as he got." George W. Bush was well-known for his fitness and athleticism. Not only did he frequently hold "heat runs" in the summer months at his ranch in Crawford, Texas, he also was fond of going off-road on his bicycle near Quantico.

"He used to go to Quantico to ride his bike. Actually, it was closer to Beltsville where the Secret Service trains. Anyway, he would go out on the ranges, and he would ride his bike with a bunch of other people. I don't know for sure, but I think it was his goal to try and lose us.

"We would be in a van with all of the equipment we needed in case of emergency. The Secret Service would be following on four wheelers and bicycles. And they would be calling into me with the grid coordinates. I had a terrain map laid out on my lap as I was driving. They would call me on the radio and let me know where they were. We would be following, and he would come flying out of the woods onto a dirt road. I would be sitting there, and he would kind of stop and look over at me like, 'How in the hell do you know where I'm at?'

"He was in such great shape. People didn't always know (this), but he was in great shape. He would invite some younger people from the White House to ride with him. We actually had a back-up van that we would use to pick them up because they couldn't keep up with him.

He would lose them. The back-up van would actually put their bikes into the back, and they would call me to ask where the President is. I told them and they would race up and drop that person off. They would take the bike out of the back of the van and the rider would jump back on and try to join right in, hoping the President didn't notice they had fallen out. They would quickly try and pedal to catch up to him and not let the President know that they had dropped out three miles back."

As one can imagine, the last day at the White House was a melancholy one for Jones. "It was hard. It was like you were leaving all of your friends, everybody that you had been with for years."

Even today, the pull of the White House is ever-present. Jones says he stays in touch with what's going on at the agency. In fact, when we talked, President Joe Biden was a day away from a visit to Pennsylvania.

"I thought about calling and finding out who was coming. If they wanted to get together. But I really don't know anybody there anymore. It's still a weird feeling knowing an event is about to take place, but not being a part of it.

"I'm going to be probably about a mile away from where the President is going to be. He's actually going to drive right by our building. So, in kind of a way, I'd like to go out there and watch it. Just be the person on the sidelines this time. But there's a part of me that says, 'you don't want to be that person that you used to get mad at.' Because there are always people in the way. I don't want to create something that would distract them from something else.

"I do miss it. I miss being around the soldiers. You know. Because we all, everybody got along, everybody. We had barbeques together. There was a bunch of us that used to carpool together in the mornings. We had motorcycles we rode together to the White House. I just miss being around all of the guys."

It is that unity and the sense of purpose that is missing in this country, Jones admits. However, he says America's best days are ahead, not behind, us.

"We probably just got into a little slump. You know, we're a great country. I mean, we can overcome anything. Now, I know there are things going on in the world right now. They are just not right. But we're going to overcome that because that's the kind of country we are. We're a better country than what's happening right now. We're a lot stronger and we're going to stay, we're going to stay strong."

CHAPTER 9

Hail to the Chef

Martin C.J. "Marti" Mongiello, Presidential Service Badge #14592

Martin Mongiello pictured at the "Inn of the Patriots" showing off his set of custom Ergo Chef Knives. (Courtesy: The US Presidential Culinary Museum.c.2020)

From being a Qualified Submarine Service Warrior to being trained as a Squad Leader in anti-terrorism by the U.S. Marine Corps to even being recognized as first in his class at the Law Enforcement Academy, you find yourself asking just who is former White House Chef Martin Mongiello (Presidential Service Badge #14592)?

"I'm a compassionate, kind, magnanimous Leo," he said as he ventures off into a soliloquy about the importance of being ethically fair and balanced.

"We are all different. We can't treat everyone the same, but we can treat everyone fairly. And that's perhaps the biggest lesson of leadership. You can't dare to treat everybody in the workforce the same. If you have a person, say Tom in a bakery and he's talking to Serge who was born and raised in Russia, but is getting his American Citizenship. You know his backstory, that his father served for 38 years in the Russian Army, and his father constantly heard soldiers complaining constantly about the food. So, by learning about Serge you know how to reach him in a different way. You talk to him differently and treat him differently. You use different forms of empathic understanding and care in your conversation.

"Conversely, if you have someone who came from the streets of Brooklyn and was arrested, but a judge gave him the choice of joining the military or going to jail, you will treat that person differently too. It's all in knowing the situation so you can get the outcome you want.

Mongiello is an accomplished public speaker who never wastes an opportunity to tell everyone that management needs to be taught, but managers also need to be willing to learn. To get there, as the leader of a Fortune 500 company or even as a parent, you have to understand that everyone is different, a separate snowflake if you will.

"A lot of parents get that. They realize that each child is different. You can't raise your daughter the way you raised yourself. And the same thing holds true when they grow up. Sometimes, you talk to one every day. You talk to the other every two and a half months. It's whatever works best for them and their needs."

Mongiello now operates The Inn of the Patriots in Grover, North Carolina, just outside Charlotte. The Inn, just steps from famed Kings Mountain Battlefield, is part of the U.S. Presidential Culinary Museum and is also home to the Presidential Service Center. It's a place that's been featured by newspaper and television outlets around the world. Considered the #1 ranked country inn in the world in the history category, The Inn of the Patriots is well-known for its service and attention to detail. Those are two things that Mongiello takes great pride in.

"Everyone is like, how do you have a 9.8 on booking.com? For six straight years? I'm like, it is all taking care of people. Sometimes, it's that one guest who calls and wants to talk for about 46 minutes. Sometimes, it's that guest that comes in with plastic bags for luggage. I tell my staff, 'Do not ever dare talk down to anyone!' I've had people who have just hit the lottery and drove to Raleigh to cash in the ticket. And they show up looking all shabby with crappy clothes on, unshaven. But you treat them like anyone else. You never know."

Mongiello's confidence is authentic and comes through in any conversation one has with him. It's a result of his years of experience as a straight shooter. In fact, even as a young boy growing up on the streets of Philadelphia, that was at his core. He knew what he wanted to be, even if how he was going to get there was still undefined.

"I always kind of knew that I wanted to be a chef. Even at a young age, I was always cooking and setting the table. I was kind of the laughingstock of my family because I would use kitchen towels as placemats. We didn't even own fancy placemats. So, I would lay out a kitchen towel, like a rectangle and put a plate down on top of it. And then, I would have all this silverware on the left and the right. I even had three glasses out there because when I watched television the place-settings had three glasses. I put apple juice in one, grape juice in another and water in the third.

"The different members of my family would come in and ask, 'Martin, what are you making tonight? Your table is decorated so nicely!'

"Growing up in Philadelphia you know, in grade school we went to see the Liberty Bell and of course, Constitution Hall with the Greenfeld tablecloths.

"It wasn't until later, that you learn about those things they don't teach you about the Revolutionary War. Until you move down south, where I am today, you don't learn that of the five-thousand or so battles in the Revolutionary War, more were fought in the south than anywhere else. And here you also learn that it wasn't until the 1950s that the first national park dedicated to that war was built south of the Mason-Dixon Line. Sometimes, it takes time to 'change history.'"

Mongiello started his effort to change history by joining the military right out of high school. He went to boot camp in San Diego then literally took his seabag and walked across the street to the Naval Training Center and cooking school. It was there that he volunteered for his new assignment, the first of many duties in which he raised his hand to accept. Assignments that made him more than just a cook.

"Someone came through recruiting for the all-volunteer nuclear submarine fleet. They stressed it was volunteer, but if you think you can handle it and after some testing, we make sure that you actually can, we can give you two things. Number one: You won't go to the fleet, you will go to nuclear submarine school in Groton, Connecticut. Number two: you will get paid extra money and you can decide where you want to be stationed. We'll give you that latitude, that chance to control your destiny.

"So, at 19, I volunteered for submarine service, the silent service. I went to Groton. We affectionately called it 'Rotten Groton.'

"Ordinarily, when a recruit arrives, you're in your company by the next morning. But I had to wait three weeks for my company to form. So, you're spending time painting lines and polishing torpedoes. They were trying to get a class of 30 or so people. Finally, we got the numbers, and they sat us all down. The Petty Officer started out by saying, 'look to your left and look to your right, because those two people aren't going to be here in two weeks. This is hard work.'

"You learn all about fusion and fission, how the nuclear primary and second loops run electrical distribution buses, it's intense. Most people can't grasp it. They'll tap out. They'll ring the bell and go to the surface fleet. Sure enough, in about two weeks, that happened. I didn't have to go to any remedial study, I was just able to pick up on it. I was lucky. I was very lucky. I had a fantastic education in high school.

"So, I went to my first submarine, the USS Sunfish. It was the first of six submarines during my career."

It was Mongiello's time on the Sunfish that he really learned how to cook. Even though he had paid his way through private high school by working at a number of restaurants, it was the non-stop atmosphere onboard a submarine that allowed him to focus on cooking as a craft.

"I never went to (a formal) culinary school. People would ask me where I learned to cook. I would tell them that I was self-taught in a sewer pipe (a submarine) with one hundred and fourteen other men."

That Navy pedigree came in handy when Mongiello was approached to work in the White House. He quickly learned that only the Navy was allowed to work in the White House mess and only the Navy was allowed to run the pair of restaurants underneath the Oval Office. This tradition has a long history. As far back as 1880, Navy stewards provided food service to the Commander in Chief. Since then, the Navy has sent the "best of its best" to man the lines, both at the White House and later at Camp David, the Presidential Retreat in Maryland.

Those restaurants, which have a waiting list of almost three months, are there to serve those in the White House, many of whom don't have the time to leave Eighteen Acres and then return for what can be a lengthy security check.

For a place as buttoned-down as the White House, Mongiello's background in law enforcement and anti-terrorism fit perfectly with his cooking experience. After all, security is always a concern when you are serving food to people in the highest level of government, including the President. So, it was not a surprise when the Secretary of the Navy nominated him to serve at the White House. It eventually took about 14 months, but he was interviewed and selected during the Administration of President George H.W. Bush. He beat out more than 50 other candidates for the position. Mongiello ended up cooking and working with six Presidents at either the White House or Camp David: (George H.W. Bush, Bill Clinton, George W. Bush, Barack Obama, Donald Trump, Joe Biden).

"I was scared to death for like the first two weeks," he said.

However, he quickly learned that they were just people, albeit hungry ones. Mongiello said there were times when you even had to protect them from themselves.

"The Presidents were my patients. The secret was that you never tell them how you made it. And you don't use any little fake names like 'Fettuccine Alfredo' because it's not. For a person like Bill Clinton, who is lactose intolerant and can't ingest wheat, how are you going to make Fettuccine Alfredo? You can't use the cheese to make the sauce and you can't have wheat in the noodles?

"So, when you go out there to answer to the First Lady about how her husband is eating something that he can't? So, even though you want to take the Chef's coat off, you keep it on. You wonder if this is the night you're going to get fired. So, I get to the table and there's Hillary and Bill and Chelsea and others, like 12 people.

I said, 'Yes, ma'am.'

She said, 'So you know, we're all eating this food and we're not having you make different food for us.'

'Was there something the matter?'

'No, but what about the cheese here? That's a whole bowl of grated cheese, Marti.'

'Oh, that's almond cheese.' The President would smile and tell everyone that he could put like 16 tablespoons of this all over his Fettucine.

'Well, Marti, what about the cream sauce? The fat-laden cream sauce? It's made with milk and butter and cheese.'

'I know how it's typically made, but I did this all with rice. This is all a rice sauce.'

"Ever since they gave me the guidelines and I've been working and studying. I'm actually inventing things on my own now. I knew what he's allowed to ingest and what he's not."

Trust grew between the Clintons and Mongiello as they each crossed paths with the other within the White House. Sometimes, it was Bill Clinton coming to the kitchen to just talk and say hi. Sometimes, it was Hillary Clinton coming down to grab a snack. They quickly got to know each other as people, not just titles. As each day passed, Mongiello found different ways to follow the health guidelines needed to protect the President.

"Now to the cheesecake story. Like I said before, you call things a different name, that's lesson number one. It wasn't really Fettuccine

Alfredo, but it was Fettuccine with a Roman Cream Sauce. Now, when it comes to cheesecake, you can't list it like tofu cheesecake because they won't touch it right? I called this cheesecake with strawberry sauce. You know, something to throw them off. They ate it and they loved it. I talked with the President later and asked him, 'Sir, if I told you that I had made the cheesecake with tofu…'

"He said, 'Honest to God, I would not (have eaten it). We love what you're doing. And it all does taste good. I guess that's how we'll do it from now on Marti. We'll eat the food and then we'll bring you out here afterwards to tell us. What an adventure.'

I was like, 'Yes, sir. It's an adventure for me too. I've never had to know how to cook medical cuisine. And this has been a great opportunity for me to learn all this.'

"They all have their favorites. Joe (Biden's) is hilarious. His favorite sandwich is called Capriotti's Bobbie. Like a Bobbie from England. It's Thanksgiving in a hoagie roll. He's got some other favorites, like ice cream. His favorite is Jenny's Ice Cream out of Ohio. I've just found these things to be fascinating and that's led to the United States Presidential Culinary Museum.

"To me, it really is all about service. If President Bush wants a honey and peanut butter sandwich, give it to him. It's not about you. Just because you've worked here for 42 years, you think you know better. You don't. They're not all like that, but there are some attitudinal dispositions that are out of control.

"It's completely unnecessary to make people feel uncomfortable. You can't hold things over people's heads with the secret fraternity and the ring and the door knock. If he (the President) wants to get his own coffee, let him."

Mongiello managed not only to do state dinners and other events at the White House, but he was also a GM at the Presidential Retreat, Camp David.

"You work, really, we all work seven days a week until one or two in the morning some days. It's just constant. There could be 100 different meetings in a day and there's a "rack and stack" in different rooms. This one could be Junior Achievement and there's two sets of winners with their parents. That could be almost 200 people. You had others that were seven minutes long with the President, then you had a meeting with the governors, say in the Indian Treaty Room. 46 were able to attend.

"Okay, what's after that? It's Mothers Against Drunk Driving. We'll bring you over to the Eisenhower building to be with them. This is taking place all day long, all night long. You can quickly see how the President would get carpal tunnel syndrome shaking all those hands.

"Then there's Camp David. You can be bartending there until 2:30 in the morning. You're obviously not wearing a white chef's coat. You change into a polo with the Camp David embroidery on it and put on some khaki pants. So, you have a rolling bar that opens up and people would just start coming to you.

"I remember one time that someone came up and I said, 'Aren't you Mr. Robbins?' He said, 'Yea, yea, just call me Tony.' I said I have your book at home, Awaken the Giant Within. He said, 'That's great!' A guest might ask, 'Do you know how to make a gin rickey?' Then the next person comes up and asks, 'How about a Golden Cadillac? Can you do one of those? And how about a Grasshopper for my wife?' You know, you have to do various jobs because that's what the role requires. You might work eighteen hours a day for seven days a week for months on end. You do it and you thank God for the privilege."

THE NO-FAIL MISSION

"It's like when you are deployed, you know it's seven days a week. There are nights when you sleep in your uniform. You would give anything for a hot shower, but you are doing what needs to be done."

Doing what needs to be done is a lesson that Mongiello, a disabled and injured Veteran, doesn't just speak of, it's one that he frequently acts on. He's known for his charitable work, which more often than not, gives him chances to connect people who need help with those who are in a position to do just that.

"I tell people that I am a jack of no trades and a master of one. And they're like, 'wait, let me write that down.' Anyway, what the one is—is publicity. I am like an endless publicity machine. Sometimes, it's all about raising awareness so you can make a difference.

"There was this guy who was blown up in his Humvee in Iraq. He needed new discs in his back. He comes home, a former Marine in Rock Hill, South Carolina. He couldn't pay his bills, so they cut off his power. Eventually, he's up in his second-floor window with a weapon. There's a SWAT team out there. There's a helicopter and he's there with his nine-millimeter. The whole PTSD thing and it was as bad as you can imagine because they plunged his home into the ice-cold darkness right before Christmas. The people in the town didn't care that everyone in his Humvee died and he was the sole survivor. He just couldn't do it anymore. After a year of working at the Post Office, he just couldn't walk anymore.

"He needed the operation, but the discs he needed weren't FDA approved and that meant the VA wouldn't do it.

"So, I got him on the radio, on television. He had articles written about him in newspapers. And one day, I got an email from the doctor who invented the discs. He was in California. He said he read about the whole thing and heard about what you are doing for this young man. 'I want to donate the discs that I invented.' He can get the operation in Germany where it's legal. He got his operation a few years ago, and I just went to his brand-new, mortgage free home that was given to him from 'Building Homes for Heroes.'

"Even today, I'm helping a young girl in India. People are like, you have never been to India and the audacity of what you are attempting to do is ridiculous in itself. I'm like, it is yeah, ridiculous, but watch. It's the right thing to do. I'm going to get this girl flown to Barcelona and she's going to get the DNA treatment she needs for her cancer."

Service is a cornerstone of what makes Mongiello tick. When he sees the service of others not being recognized for what it is, it rubs him the wrong way.

"I think there's a huge disconnect. For some, there is animosity toward returning veterans who wear medals that shine and glint in the sunlight. Then there are those who celebrate their service. Those are very difficult for some in the service to get over. That's why there are veterans who would rather live in the woods and say, 'I just don't fit in.'

"There's a sheer disconnect about what the military is really all about. I mean, we have a lot of people who come home, and people say, 'let's get Shaniqua to join us. She served our country.' Then others say 'Whoa, we can't do that, we don't want no blacks.' It's hard to believe what's going on.

"When you go away to the military, it's all blended, religion too. There are non-denominational services and if you're on a big enough ship, you can have a Jewish service or a Muslim service. I knew an Imam, and before services people would go up to the navigator and ask which direction was Mecca. They would go out on the weather deck and face starboard or port, whichever way was Mecca. The Jewish Rabbi would come in and then would clear the room, and the Catholics would have their mass. It's just the way it was."

Mongiello's first 'on-land' duty station was at the Pensacola Naval Air Station. At just the age of 22, he helped to manage a fifteen-hundred room hotel on base. He was also tasked with making sure events at the Air Station, such as a visit from the Blue Angels, went smoothly. For that he needed even more training.

"It was pretty wild. I mean, you know, it's not only the Blue Angels, but they would have huge music acts and other acts come into the Pensacola Naval Air Station.

"The Marine Corps was going to be stationed on every naval base. This was the late 80s. They were going to ramp up and staff up with an auxiliary security force made up of sailors. So, I volunteered to become a squad leader for an anti-terrorism squad. I was trained by the Marine Corps. Part of that was not only doing security and bodyguard duties for all the bands and musical acts, but literally anything else that came to town. Say there was a huge air show, they would roll out the auxiliary security force and I would be a part of that. But that wasn't all.

"Sometimes, we got up in the middle of the night. There was one time when a stray Tomahawk (missile) flew off the range at Elgin Air Force Base. It landed in a farmer's field and cracked in half. Fuel was all over the place. We had to go out there immediately in the pitch-black to secure the whole area until EOD could come in. You put your camos on and that's what you would go do."

It wouldn't seem that issues of safety and security would follow Mongiello during his career as a chef at both the White House and Camp David. However, they were never far from the events, and sometimes the economic realities, of the day.

"It seems like some presidents think they can reduce the White House staff. Bill Clinton tried it, John F. Kennedy tried it, even Donald Trump. Trump made some negative comments about Camp David, but they all quickly understand the value of Camp David and the fact that "Orange One" is located underground there.[1] It's a nuclear-hardened facility. It's designed as a secondary launch platform for whoever's last. Cheney went there during 9/11 when they flew Bush out west. We didn't know what was going to happen next with 9/11. So, they put Bush in his own bunker out west."

"(Orange One) is just one of those places. I know that Biden's already been briefed and ready. (On a side note,) one thing that people are deflated to learn when I tell them is that the Nuclear Briefcase (football) actually doesn't have a retinal scanner. There is no, you know, protective case that you flip up. There's no glowing red button that the president presses to launch. There's not a palm scanner in there. All the types of stuff that people have mentioned to me. They say their cousin once carried the football. Then, I'm like, 'well, if that's what he told you, he's wrong.' Let's call his Colonel right now. I don't want to start a family incident, but I'm like I don't think he ever told you that. There's nothing in there but manilla folders."

Interspersed between his time at the White House and Camp David, Mongiello had various cooking assignments abroad. In Japan, he cooked for Prime Minister Ryutaro Hashimoto, who led that country from 1996 to 1998. He also cooked for King Abdullah and his wife Queen Rania of Jordan. He cooked in Brussels at NATO. One of his teams won the International Food Service Executives Association

---

1 Existence of "Orange One" revealed in a number of resources including:

Gulley, Bill (1980). Breaking Cover. Simon and Schuster. p. 150. ISBN 0671245481.

Nelson, Dale (2000). The President is at Camp David. Syracuse University Press. pp. 38–39. ISBN 0815606281. "Camp David". Dwight Eisenhower Presidential Library. National Archives and Records Administration

Wright, Lawrence (2015). Thirteen Days in September: The Dramatic Story of the Struggle for Peace. Knopf Doubleday. p. 63. ISBN 0804170029.

(IFSEA) Captain Edward F. Ney World Award for the Best Restaurant in the World. He also represented the Navy on NBC's Today Show.

"There was a competition held in New York City. It was held on board the Intrepid. The Marines, Coast Guard, Navy, Air Force—all the services. My team won that year. And the reward, for the first time in history, you have got to go on the Today Show. And the Today Show put 'Best Chef in the Armed Forces' under my name. It was interesting being there with Katie Couric and Lester Holt."

While living in Europe, Mongiello was knighted as he was welcomed into the Order of St. Thomas More IACK. One would think that just receiving the honor would be reward enough, but during the ceremony itself, Mongiello had something else on his mind.

"It was kind of unbelievable. I was waiting for an 'arise, Sir Martin.' But what was really going through my head was 'don't cut me with that thing.' I know it's bad, but in all honesty, you're kneeling and there's a person standing with a sword on your shoulders and they're going back and forth. Really, all you can think of is 'please don't cut me.' Seriously. Please don't cough or slip or something. That's what I was really thinking."

Today, Mongiello continues to give back, not just in the United States, but around the world to draw attention to various causes including the fight against hunger. He's worked with orphanages on three continents. Stateside, he helped raise 567-thousand dollars in one night for Cystic Fibrosis by serving dinner to more than 300 people. He's also got his attention focused on helping those veterans succeed back here in the states.

"After World War II, 54 percent of the veterans who came home were able to open up their own businesses. Today, it's just 4 percent. That has to change."

CHAPTER 10

One team, one fight

Seth Rawson, Presidential Service Badge #19798

Photo of Seth Rawson on board the Presidential Aircraft, n.d. (Photo from Seth Rawson)

"If the White House called again, I would be on the first plane, instantly, no questions asked. Doesn't matter to me who the President is. You are doing it for the Republic, not for the person."

For ET2 Seth Rawson, his time at the White House was memorable. Being a recipient of the Presidential Service Badge (#19798) was a career milestone and one that he will always cherish.

"Civilians and military people see different things when we look at dress uniforms. For the military, when you have a device insignia like the PSB, it's a standout thing. Not a lot of people have it and when it includes the Presidential seal, it's special. Mine is as pristine today as it was the day that I was given it. That's been almost twenty years. That's how significant it continues to be to me today.

"It's not canonized in our culture like the way a Purple Heart is or a Medal of Honor or a Presidential Medal of Freedom. Those are big things and are rightfully so. They are very limited in their distribution. They require significant sacrifice. The PSB requires sacrifice and dedication as well."

That sacrifice and dedication manifests itself in different ways; depending on the role that one has in support of the President and the office. That role can also feature something that many Americans have dealt with in recent years, how to keep up with the growth in technology.

"When I was there, the White House transitioned from analog to digital radio. That was a whole different type of technology base. It was a huge challenge because the architecture and infrastructure covered the Secret Service, the military, and the Presidential staff. That's a big deal."

Rawson came to the White House from his duty station in Italy where he worked in a building that was essentially underground. The only visible sign that anything was there were the radio antennas on the roof. During his time there, Rawson helped to oversee a variety of projects, including providing radio triangulation for space shuttles. One day, his commander approached him about a new mission.

"I was told, 'We have selected you as the top performing person of this command. You are the best among the best. We would like to know if you would like to be interviewed for a chance to work at the White House?'

"My response was sure, yes, absolutely!

"You knew there were going to be challenges and difficulties at that operational level. You knew you were going to be pushed. If you are the type of person who wants to feel that push and to expand, to get that knowledge set that you need to be successful, you are going to strive for that type of position.

"Within that room there were a couple of people, like me, who were very interested. There were others who turned it down. They wanted to stay overseas, or they didn't want to go to Virginia. Whatever their personal reasons were, they said no.

"So, I was selected, or I volunteered, I guess I should say. I was interviewed for about an hour. They asked me technical questions of course, but they also asked emotional intelligence questions and moral questions. Like, if you were faced with this kind of situation, what you would do?

"I remember those questions because I thought, 'Man, no one has ever really asked me these kinds of questions.' It struck me as strange. No decision was made following the interview. I guess they were travelling through the different commands in Europe looking for the right people to come into the White House command."

Rawson headed back from the White House three months later. He received a letter saying he had been selected to serve the "Office of the President" in whatever capacity was required. As with others who had made this journey in the past, the FBI began a deep dive into his past, speaking with friends and family over the years.

"I told them, 'No, no, I'm not in trouble. They are just doing a background investigation. It's standard.'"

Those questions that Rawson faced in the interview process as well as the other checks and balances that he and his friends and family participated in helped him as he advanced in his career. When he transitioned to the civilian world, he found that many of those experiences translated well to that environment and to the people he wanted to hire for his company.

"When I interview people, the more I find myself trying to understand people. I often spend time asking technical or job-specific questions. I have found myself trying to get the sense of the person. If I think the person is a good person, if I feel they can do the job and have the drive and desire to do it, then it's just a matter of me putting the right tools and the right training in their hands. So, I try to assess the person. Does the person fit in? Do they fit the culture, the tempo, the long-term goals? And I think the questions that I was asked all those years ago were similar. They were trying to assess the person.

"There was one question that pitted my life against humanity, that type of question. It was something like, if you knew the world could harvest your body and save a million lives, would you let it happen? What if you had to make that decision today?

"I'm like yeah, I'd do that. Because I feel if we're talking about a million people there has to be a few standouts there that are going to be worth it, right?

"That just seemed like such a weird question to ask somebody because we went from asking me questions on directional radiation of antennas to this hypothetical question. It kind of stuck with me."

Rawson cleared the background check process and found himself packing up to leave Italy for the environs of the Washington DC metro area. Even though he was heading home, it was still a culture shock, and in more ways than one.

"I hadn't been to the states in six years, so they were a memory to me. I just wasn't very familiar with things because I had spent a great deal of time overseas. I just never went back. I remember that when I left Italy that I had a three-bedroom apartment with marble floors. It was two floors over a bakery. It had a front and back wraparound balcony that took up most of the building's front. The building was five stories high. My landlord lived underneath me. She was fantastic. She was an old Italian lady who would make me food and randomly put in front of my door. At that time, I was just a single guy and not the best cook in the world. That place cost me about $450 a month.

"So, I got to Alexandria Virginia and found a one-bedroom, a real small apartment and ended up paying about $1100 a month. I remember how crazy that was. The next shock I got was the traffic. Beltway traffic, I don't miss it! If I didn't make it across the Woodrow Wilson Bridge by 6:50am, my commute time doubled. So that was my goal, essentially."

But it wasn't just the commute. Rawson found himself back in Washington around the time of the infamous DC sniper attack. During three weeks in October 2002, there were a series of shootings in the region. Ten people were killed. Three others were wounded. John Allen Muhammad and Lee Boyd Malvo were arrested after they were found sleeping in a car at a Frederick County, Maryland rest stop. They were eventually tried and convicted of the shootings. Muhammad was sentenced to death and was executed seven years later. Malvo was sentenced to life in prison. To arrive in the DC area during this time of fear and uncertainty was unnerving, even for a professional soldier like Rawson.

"I was like, 'is this a real thing right now? Is this real?' It makes you want to go back to Italy right away. I mean, what are the odds at this moment, at this time, when I'm going to work at the White House? And the thing I have to think about is, 'am I going to randomly be shot when I park my car? Is that something that's going to happen?' I know there's so many people in the Metro DC area and the odds of that happening are astronomically small. But you know, we're humans. We're not rational humans, right? We still think about it and the rationality goes out the window when you see a report of a random shooting."

For Rawson, that report time eventually came. Like so many others, his "first day" wasn't at the White House but over at the Anacostia Annex, a short distance away. It was there that he learned the ins and outs of the massive operation that supported the Office of the President. He learned how things worked. He received his credentials. And he got to learn more about the people with whom he would be working with, some closely, at his new duty station.

"I remember my first day. I walked in and walked around the exterior of the building trying to find out where I needed to go. I'm walking around and I come to this giant loading dock. There are three or four or five tractor trailers pulled up to this loading dock. Case after case after case is being moved by hand, by pallet. There are dozens of people moving all of this around. I eventually found the guy I needed to see and asked him what was going on. He was like, 'Well you know, these guys are loading. Those guys are unloading. This is all for a trip.' I said, 'It must be a huge trip.' It was actually a one-day stopover. The President was going to New Mexico or wherever. But all these people were working to get the right equipment for the right truck in the right place while receiving all of this other equipment that was coming back. All of that equipment had to be checked and validated and other things done to it to make sure nothing happened to it, or if it was compromised on the trip. All of these things were happening at that point in time and I'm looking at that.

"I'm thinking that I can't believe all this happens for just a single trip. I mean, this is one trip. I will tell you that after I learned that this was the tiniest exposed part of that iceberg. When you're associated with the President, people don't understand all the work that goes into that, except for the people who are involved in the operations every day.

"It's not just having the right equipment in the right place, you have to have the right people in the right places, too. That's such an important part of it all. There are so many things that have to happen before the President gets on Air Force One out of Andrews Air Force Base. There are just so many things that happen before he steps on that stairway. There must be perfect execution. That's not to say there are no mistakes. But the mistakes that happen are corrected in real time, almost instantaneously, almost seamlessly. Because you can't really have mistakes, right? Because it reflects back on the office. You don't have mistakes. You don't. There's no such thing as 'we couldn't.' That doesn't exist."

That desire for perfection, even the rapid elimination of mistakes, adds to both the mystique and the very real stress that comes with serving the Office of the President. It's a job that's not for everyone, Rawson readily admits. However, for those who can handle it, it can be rewarding.

"Is it good stress? I imagined the stress that someone like Michael Phelps feels when he's training, knowing that the weeks lead up to the Olympics. That's good stress, right? It motivates you. It pressures you. It pushes you to do better. In that sense, it's good stress. But I will tell you that along with good stressors, there are bad stressors, too. I saw a lot of people, who because of operational tempo or mission requirements saw their family, their home live really affected by and really hurt by it.

"I made a commitment that when I joined the military that I was never going to get married until I was out of the military. And I made that commitment after I had been in the military for probably about three years. It was just a constant thing in the military. The pressures were so next level and the pressures that this puts on a family, I didn't think it would be fair for me to have a family and expect them to have to share in that pressure and be able to succeed through it. I didn't think that was a fair expectation. There are plenty of families that do it and do succeed. But there are plenty of families that don't."

The numbers themselves only tell part of the story. During the 2004 election year, Rawson was on the road with President George W. Bush 289 days out of 365. That can play havoc with a person's personal life, to be sure. That sheer volume of work gave Rawson a renewed respect for those who hold the office. He knew that if he was feeling the pressure to perform, that the President was as well, but at a whole different level.

"Is there any other job that can compare? You have to be, quite literally, all things to all people. There are going to be people that, no matter what you do, you are not going to make happy. And there are going to be people that, no matter what you do, you are going to make happy. But the overarching responsibility of the President is to be accountable to the American people.

"I don't think there's anything more fulfilling than making sure the President can have that accountability and be there for the people. I mean, when you are supporting the President and making sure that he is able to get the things done that he has to get done, you are supporting the country. You understand the ramifications of the mission and what it means for America. I think that's for military service at large, but especially at the White House. I don't know if I can think of anything that would be better to do."

That desire for service was honed as Rawson grew up in New York state. In scouting, he learned the importance of honor, commitment, and courage.

"That is probably where those core values really started to be more than just words to me. I never quite got to Eagle Scout."

By his own admission, Rawson was poor. He called it "food kitchen poor." He eventually left scouting to help to support his mother. He worked jobs during his junior and senior year of high school so they could stay in their home, and he could stay at his high school.

"I don't regret not getting it (Eagle Scout). I think I did the right thing for the right reasons at the right time. It was just a different time and a different type of trial. My mom loved me very much and years later I left the White House to take care of her again. As a single parent and an only child, you either make it together…or you don't make it. We made it through every day."

That hardscrabble existence growing up left Rawson compassionate for the challenges that others face, but he admits that it's hard to balance that with the needs of his business.

"I sometimes sit back and tell my team, 'We're going to be pushing very hard.' Sometimes I hear, 'I'm so tired and this and that.' I tell them that I'm going to be very honest with them because of who I am and what I've lived through in my life. I know as a personal shortfall; it can be hard for me to hear somebody talk about how hard things are. But I also have the emotional intelligence to know that nobody in this room is me. We all experience pain or feel differently. My first instinct when you say it's too hard, my first instinct for myself is to say, try harder. Try until you know, for sure, that it's absolutely impossible. Because I think impossible is very, very, very, very, very far away from where we are now. That doesn't mean I don't hear what you're saying. But it is difficult for me to say, and that's probably my first inclination to say, well, it's probably not that hard."

It's also not hard for Rawson to connect with his former peers at the White House. He was part of an exclusive group charged with serving the Office of the President. He is still close to many of them even though they served many years ago.

"The vast majority of the people that I served with at the White house are very happy, very successful, very highly motivated, very energetic, very high functioning people. They are doing things they want to do now. There's one guy that I worked with who lives out in Lake Tahoe and he's a handyman. He's very happy doing his own thing. He has plenty of time for himself and there's nothing wrong with that. Whatever gives you balance in life. That's the thing. That's what I mean by high functioning. They're happy with where they're at and what they're doing."

In addition to his stateside assignments, serving the Office of the President took Rawson around the world. As you can imagine, there were always challenges amid the beauty of these different countries. Many times, detailed planning can go out the window because of something unexpected. That's where the ability to pivot and adapt becomes crucial, even amid the "crazy" as Rawson recalls during a trip to St. Petersburg, Russia.

"That story starts the moment we touched down. It's a long flight from Andrews to Russia. We stop in Guam and then move from Guam to Russia. We've got the vehicles, the Presidential limos, all of the equipment, everything. We land and we get everything on vehicles that the embassy had ready for us. We take the limo straight to the embassy because that's the only place that it can be parked.

"So, we start unloading all of the equipment, taking inventory because we want to make sure that we have the same number of boxes in St. Petersburg that we had at Andrews. Then, we get to the hotel, and we unload them all, and we count them again. That's when we find out that we're missing two base radio stations.

"Nobody has any idea where these radios are, they're gone. This is a big deal. I can tell you that we have never lost equipment on any other trip at any given time at any location anywhere else in the world. So, we let the embassy know instantly. This is becoming a really big deal. So those at the embassy reached out to their contacts in the Russian government. The Russian government reached out to the FSB (the successor to the KGB).

"Within fifteen minutes, we got a phone call. We went outside the hotel to one of the trucks that we had locked up. Both of those station radios were inside.

"We're like great! Nobody will ever know that something happened. Were they there the whole time or were they moved? It's crazy. Literally crazy. We didn't want to have to cancel the Presidential trip because people were playing with classified equipment. We didn't want to have to spend 30 or 40 million on new equipment because our technology and our chip classification has all been compromised.

"So, we reached back out to DC and said, 'Look, we need more Marines out here because we need to put 24-hour guard on everything we're doing here.' We can't play games. The one thing we aren't going to compromise on is our communications.

"It was still two weeks before the visit. While we did get a marine detail to protect this stuff, we were still keeping an eye on the

THE NO-FAIL MISSION

equipment ourselves. That meant we were doing double duty. We had to build the infrastructure to coordinate the phone lines, to coordinate the satellite to go out to all these remote stations while also keeping a watch on the equipment. It quickly becomes 'when can we get back to Andrews?'

"This is a huge challenge because what people may or may not realize is that when the President goes anywhere, all the Secret Service and all the military and all of the staff have radios. Those radios are heard all the way in DC no matter where the event is. So, you need receiving stations that are built from scratch each time. You have to be able to take this radio frequency and transmit it through encrypted phone lines. Basically, whatever it takes to get it to the other side. So, whenever someone pushes a button on location, they can hear them all the way in DC. And anybody who's in the region can hear them, no matter what. Think about that. The entire architecture for a trip is built in less than five days.

"That's continually being done, being taken down and being created again. Multiply that by the trips. It's the same thing for the Vice-President. It's the same thing for others as directed by the President. It starts to add up."

Add up, it does. Especially when you consider that the President is often in more than one location during these visits, and he has to get from point A to point B. That means at every step of the journey everyone has to have constant contact with the President and his support staff. Without it, there could be areas where the President is exposed and at risk.

"We go out to these locations, and we do site surveys. We say, 'Okay, we think this is a good location. We've got a bit of height. This will work.'

"So, on this Russian trip, we determined that one of the places we wanted as a site was this really old, dilapidated schoolhouse. And this is where things get interesting.

"We had made a decision earlier that we were going to lock up all of our passports at the hotel and bring a paper copy with us. That's because we all had diplomatic passports. They are extremely hard to replace. It seemed like a good idea, right?

"So, let me paint this scene for you. The schoolhouse is two stories. Some of the windows are broken out. It looks like when you see the videos of nature reclaiming the buildings around Chernobyl. That's what this schoolhouse looks like. I mean, it hasn't had people there in years. The inside is old and filled with dust. We get to the top of this thing, and we have poles and base stations and radios. We've got handheld radios and brick phones and all kinds of stuff, all of this equipment that we are bringing with us.

"We start putting together these giant antennas and we're securing them to the room, using what we call 100 mile-per-hour tape to hold them down, so they don't sway. This is a lot of work and there's just three of us. We get hungry. Our translator says, 'No problem. I'm going to drive up the road. There's a little place like eight or ten miles away where I'll get some sandwiches and some drinks and bring them back.' So, he leaves.

"Seven minutes later, a cop car pulls up. These two Russian police officers get out. They probably got a call saying there are three people at the school who do not look like locals. And they know there are a bunch of big wigs coming through town in a couple of days. So, they're suspicious.

"I tell my guys, 'Listen, everyone be cool. Everyone put everything down.' We're going to sit down over here because they were walking toward the building. It was a brisk walk. It's not like they were running but certainly not out for a Sunday stroll either.

"Everyone is just real calm. We know that we have encrypted stuff and other things. I said, 'If we're going to get arrested, if anything goes wrong, or if we know something's going wrong, drop the code. Instantly, drop the code. That means we're going to purge the code out of the devices and just get rid of them.'"

The act of "dropping the code" helps to ensure the safety of the equipment and the security of the team, including the President. This is material that you don't want falling into the wrong hands.

"So, these cops come on up to us and they're asking questions. Nobody understands anything or anyone. I don't know why, but as a human when we speak with someone who doesn't understand our language, we start speaking slower. Like that's going to help. Then we speak slowly and loudly. That doesn't help either and it just makes people more irritated.

"We're trying to say, 'Look over there, my bag. I've got passports in the bag.' I keep saying, 'passport, passport, passport.' I start walking toward the bag. These guys both draw their guns on us. So, we dropped the code, which is a big deal. It's a really big deal. I tell everyone to be cool, just whatever they want to do, right? We don't have anything on us except these photocopies of our passport. And if you know anything, a photocopy of a passport is just about worthless.

"They get us all together. One guy starts putting handcuffs on us. The other guy keeps his gun on us as they walk us down the stairs. They're talking on a radio. I don't know what's going on, but we get down the stairs and they stand us on the edge of the road. We've got our handcuffs on and every time we do anything, they point the guns at us. So, everyone's being really quiet. Then a paddy wagon pulls up. I'm like, this can't be a real thing that is happening. Is this really happening right now? I told the guys right there, 'Don't get in the wagon. Don't get in the wagon.'

"Because I don't know where the wagon is going. I don't know. Is this another FSB thing? Or is this a real police mistake? I don't know right now and I'm not willing to take that risk with these guys. Because this could be, you know, we go into this wagon, and we are just three people that went AWOL and no one ever sees us again. You never come back. So, what is it, right? How do you make that calculation? Is it worth it right now? So, the guys start loading me into the wagon. I'm the first one. And I was like, here we go. Here we go. So, I'm pushing with my feet there and he grabs me. I start kicking. I won't let him put me in. I won't let him put me in. This struggle goes on for a while. It felt like ten minutes, but realistically, it was probably like two- or three-minutes tops.

"At one point, the guy takes his pistol, and he hits me in the forehead with it. I have this beautiful scar where he hit me right in the middle of my forehead from being pistol-whipped.

"So, I'm bleeding all over my face and I'm stunned when they put me in the paddy wagon. They're loading another guy in there and he's fighting too. I wouldn't say I was beaten senseless, but it was pretty close. I'm with it, but not with it. I'm woozy and bleeding all over the place. I can't see because the blood is in my eyes. It's a disaster right now.

"That's when, out of nowhere, this sleek Alfa Romeo pulls up. And possibly the largest police officer that I've ever seen in my life gets out of this car and I mean large, not heavy, but a big strong man. He was just big, like your quintessential big Russian dude with the big mustache.

"He starts screaming. I don't know what's being said. He's just screaming at this guy. And the cop that hit me with the pistol says something back to him. And they're shouting at one another. That's when this big guy from the Alfa Romeo punches the other cop so hard in the face that he knocks him out. Dropped the guy right there.

"Seconds later, the handcuffs are coming off. And we're all sitting there. The guy gives me some water. Another guy comes in with a little medical kit and tries to clean me up. About five minutes later, our translator comes back. This big Russian guy tells him, 'I'm so sorry for the misunderstanding. I'm so sorry.' He must have apologized like 100 times.

"So, it ended when he got all of us taken care of. He asked about the food we were eating, that our translator had gotten for us, and he said, 'I'm going to have some food brought over. When we got back to the hotel, there was a huge delivery of Russian pastries and other things waiting for us. It was his way of saying he was sorry.

"I'm thinking after the whole thing went down that no one is ever going to know that this happened. The President is going to get here. He's going to be in his motorcade. Everything is going to go flawlessly in St. Petersburg. He's going to shake hands and everything's going to be fine. He's going to go to his Presidential Suite for the night. He's going to sleep. He's going to wake up and he's going to get back on Air Force One.

"I don't know if the President drove by that schoolhouse. I didn't want him to know. I did tell my superiors, but really, what more could be done? We had a doctor on the trip. He checked me out. I was fine to go and the next morning I woke up and me and my team went and did something that was much, much quieter."

Rawson found himself in the hospital following another overseas trip, this time to Africa. He was there providing support for President Bush as he visited Botswana in July of 2003. It was the third of five nations that the President and the First Lady visited across Africa on this trip. The visit there was focused on increasing trade between the United States and Botswana, which was one of Africa's richest countries at the time. Botswana was known for its large diamond reserves. While there, the Bushes visited the Mokolodi Nature Reserve which was home to endangered white rhinos and orphaned elephants.

"Botswana is probably one of the nicest places I've been. It's a beautiful place, the Savannah and the wilderness areas are spectacular. The food's a little weird. We did eat white rice with grubs and some other stuff while we were there. I ate some other local foods that maybe I'll never eat again. But you know, it wasn't bad."

Rawson recalls the Botswana trip as being rather quiet, at least at the outset. Being just one location out of five, a number of teams from the White House were at each location making sure the Office of the President had what it needed, when it needed it.

"It was like any other overseas trip. We got there two weeks in advance. We were going to get done what needed to get done. We're going to have a mission that's successful. But at the end of that trip, I got really, really, really sick. I got so sick that when we landed back at Andrews Air Force Base that they took me immediately to the hospital and put me in isolation. Everyone who was on that flight with me, they put in isolation. I was hallucinating. It was crazy. But I think the reason why I got so sick, and I'm not a big person for getting sick, but I think the reason why I got so sick was because the stress levels on that trip were just unbelievable. I mean there was one point in time where I don't think that I slept for three or four days."

Situations like that speak to the need of not just being able to 'read and react' in real time, but also to be able to have scenarios sketched out in advance, even if they don't come to pass. Even though you can't plan for every scenario, you do need to be able to read what's happening and then react with split-second timing.

"It does mess you up when you think about it. I try to put myself in the mindset of what our police officers deal with all the time.

"We look at the Capitol (January 6, 2021). We look at how that could have gone a totally different way. If the people in the security force there had truly escalated things. It could have been a disaster. It could have easily gone the other way. What are those officers feeling? Just imagine being the officer who watched one of your friends get beaten with an American flag, an American flag. And then, having that gun on your hip. What's going through your mind? What's going through your mind is what's next.

"So, you have that same mentality. If you have something happen that precedes a Presidential visit, you know there's intent there. Deadly intent. This is not somebody who wants to bake you a cupcake. So, you are hyper alert. You are always worried. You are always looking at people, anyone you don't know. You don't know your risk. No matter what you're doing, the entire time you are there, there's a risk. And you have to stay with it. You have to hold it together. You can't be that guy, who at that moment, decides you saw their hand move a certain way. You can't throw him to the ground. You can't be that guy because that's an international incident.

"So, I have a lot of sympathies for some escalations of force because when you're on that wire and you're walking that wire, when do you know if it's shaking too much? You're not going to know. How certain are you, really? And if you get to the place where you're certain did you now just wait too long?

"I had a conversation with my military buddies a short time ago and we talked about this. I can't remember, during my entire time of service, ever having somebody that accidentally discharged a gun. I can't remember having somebody shoot somebody who wasn't a clear and present danger. I don't remember it happening. Maybe it happened. And maybe I didn't know about it. Unlikely, but maybe.

"When you think about that, and I think the reason for that is the consequences. I can't speak to law enforcement or any private security forces, but I know in the military, if you accidentally discharged or if you kill somebody who wasn't supposed to be killed, the consequences are life-ending. So, there's no room for error. If you shoot and kill a non-enemy combatant, that's a straight trip to Leavenworth. In many cases, the court martial is just a formality."

As Rawson looks forward to what he hopes is a long professional career in civilian life, the lessons he learned at the White House frame his daily activities. He puts his faith in others, which he calls "our greatest strength." As for our greatest weakness, you might be surprised.

"I think our greatest weakness is that we feel tremendously. When I say that I mean because sometimes, right or wrong, true or false, whatever the justification in our mind that exists, that subconscious emotional investment, is huge.

"When I say it's our greatest strength, it's because I think that people have that feeling, when it's on the line, when it really matters, I believe we come together as a people. I mean, look at us after 9/11, right? Look at us, after the disasters. Look at who we are as a people after a disaster. Again, and again. Look at who we were as a country during and after World War II. Everyone's suffered. We've stretched the workforce to the absolute limits of its capabilities. You look at who we were as a people in that moment. And you contrast that with who we are as a people now. Does that same blood run through us? Do we still feel the same way about each other? If there was a true tragedy and I mean, a true tragedy, an unthinkable, unimaginable, catastrophic occurrence in which we knew we either got through it together or not at all. In my mind, we get through it together. The stuff that we're doing now, is just, the way we think now is. That mettle hasn't been tested. We've been very comfortable for a long time.

"That's not to say that we don't face tests right now. But we are being tested in different ways. You can't say there is no racism because there is. You can't say there's income equality because there's not. I think we get lost in those details and that's where our great struggle is right now. How do we come together? We have these lives that we lead and it's all I can do as the leader of an organization to tell my people that there's no red and no blue, there's just us. That's straight out of my military background. We are here for each other and so I don't want to hear anybody bashing anybody. I don't want to hear any of that. Because at the end of the day, the only people that you're going to be able to rely on if you're out there trying to get a job done is the guy with you.

"That's why I sign my emails, 'one team, one fight.' That fight is fighting for each other to be successful. Our fight is doing what we need to do for each other every day and if our organization is successful, it's because we work hard for each other."

In the end, it all comes down to those lessons that he learned as he was being raised in upstate New York. Lessons that were amplified during his time in Scouting and later in the military and at the White House.

"Why do I do this? I love my country. I love my country and I love the people in my country. You know, I used to tell people back when I was in the military who asked me why? Why are you doing this? You can do whatever you want. Why do you do that in the military? My answer was always, 'I do it because I can.' When I say that, it's because I know I can do it. And I know that if it gets hard or if I have problems that I can deal with that. It's within my capacity to do it and I do it for the people who are not able to do it. I do it for the people who don't want to do it. I love the people in this country. I love people. A lot of people who work here (The White House) have more belief in those around them than they have in their own selves.

"And that's it. That's why I would do it again. I think it's one of the greatest things you can do. I don't know that there's anything… humanitarian work stuff like that is great stuff. It's a great thing. My wife is in the medical profession, it's great stuff. Being a teacher, great stuff. I think some of us do the things we do because we know we can do them. We do them because there are people who won't. Hopefully, there are more that would than would not."

EPILOGUE

Thank you for taking the time to read the stories of these silent sentinels, those men and women who played a role, both small and large, in supporting the Office of the President, many times on the world's biggest stage. In each of my conversations with these Presidential Service Badge recipients, I posed a question: "What lessons did you learn during your time at the White House that could be applied to our society today?"

It was a question that drew humble reflection and forthright responses. For these men and women, their role in support of the Office was not political. If anything, it was far from it. Those alliances were always "checked at the door" because nothing mattered more than the mission itself. As you have learned in each of their stories, failure was not an option. The mission had to succeed, no matter the hour, no matter the exhaustion, no matter the challenge. Success was measured in a variety of different ways, but none more important than ensuring the President had what he needed, when he needed it.

"I think that as a people, our greatest strength and our greatest weakness is that we feel tremendously," said Seth Rawson. "When I say that we feel tremendously is our greatest weakness, I say that because sometimes, right or wrong, true or false, whatever the justification in our mind, our subconscious emotional investment in it is huge. And when I say it's our greatest strength, it's because I think that people have that feeling. They're patriotic. When it's on the line, when it really matters, I believe we come together as a people.

"I think we are being tested right now. But we are being tested in different ways. Right, like you can recognize there's some problems now. Our great struggle is to come together with each other.

"All I can do as a leader of an organization during the last election was to tell the people that, look, there is no red and there's no blue, there's just the people. We are here for each other, so I don't want to hear anybody bashing anybody. I don't want to hear any of that. Right? Because at the end of the day, the only person that you're going to be able to rely on if you're out there trying to get a job done is that guy who's with you. We have to realize that, yes, it is 'we the people.'"

Colonel Jeff Worthington (U.S. Army Ret.) picked up on that comment, "I do think that the loudest voices are being heard and it's being portrayed as being everything. And it may not be you. Whether it's the silent majority that may be out there, I do believe that many people, especially this younger generation does want to serve. I just hope it's the right service. I do believe, though, and it's a personal feeling, that everybody should do something to give back to their nation or to others. Because I think you learn a lot from doing that. You take care of others before you take care of yourself. Now, I like the way some countries do it, you have to complete some sort of compensatory service. I'm not advocating for this, but is there some sort of compensatory service before you finish college? I do like things like the Peace Corps where you do something for others, because I think you become a better, more whole person. And you see the world through a different lens. So, I do believe that's out there."

Rob Cole agreed, "I think we'll get back there. I think it's going to take time. You know, it's almost like we unleashed a genie of some sort. We've got to figure out how to get the genie back in the bottle."

Putting that genie back in the bottle starts, at least from some perspectives, refocusing our attention on service and making the most of any and all opportunities that we face.

"I used to pray every day when I went home and put my head on the pillow," said Erica Cooper. "Please don't let me do anything to ruin this opportunity. Because to me, it was the best opportunity in the entire world. And so, it was on so many levels, what the Presidential Service Badge means. Yes, you are supporting the President of the United States, but you are doing so much more. You're showing honor to the military branch that you're attached to. We're showing honor to the White House Communications Agency who allowed you to be a part of them. You are supporting your team member. You're showing them support through your actions. And the fact that you received the badge, and you are capable of receiving the badge, it shows that you have what it takes to stand beside them and help them to be successful."

Fellow Presidential Service Badge recipient Ivan Lagares agreed. "You always got to get the mission done. For us, there is no red or blue. There's not. When (George W.) Bush took over, there were a lot of people that were with his father. So, they were familiar with who we are. They respected you. They take your hand, and they tell you, 'Thank you for what you do.' They already know who you are. Yeah. They know the mission is going to get done regardless."

Ray Flores, who served the Office of the President during Barack Obama's tenure echoed those sentiments. "You're looking at, you know, the greatest country in the world and the most powerful person in the world. Zero failure. If something goes wrong, it's a huge embarrassment. And it ripples, and it's a part of history. So, yeah, it's totally zero failure. You have one shot. It's not like that where you have different conflicts and battles, things that go on. You fail at this, it's forever.

If you are not humble, if you are not there for the greater cause, then definitely, it will totally destroy a person."

That humility is something that Hervy "James" Oxendine mentioned more than once in our conversations.

"I think it's important to know that it takes a lot of talent. It takes a lot of work. But every individual, they are very humble. They realize how lucky they were to be able to participate in something that not only meant a lot to them but contributed a lot to the success of the country on the world scene. When you support the president, you help to provide the voice of the president to the world."

Those who have read these stories have learned that those who wear the Presidential Service Badge had a habit of putting service over self, something that many people believe has been lost in this "me-first capture it in a selfie" world.

"I guess that I hope the folks who are reading this, what they would take away from it is that we didn't do it for recognition," Jonée Coleman said. "We did it for the mission, for the goal of serving the office. We are just like other members of the military. We just did something a little different. It was still special nonetheless."

Their stories are special. The American story is their story. Men and women who came from hardscrabble backgrounds and rose to success. In this case, they ended up serving the Office of the President. To a person, they had never imagined growing up in their small towns, meager apartments, or trailer parks that they would be so integral to America and our nation's policies.

Those policies differ depending on the party in power, but at their heart they speak about the goodness of America.

In 1964, Ronald Reagan delivered a speech on such a topic. It was an address that came to be one of his more famous speeches. With just days to go in that Presidential campaign, the state Republican party in California asked Reagan to speak on behalf of the party's standard bearer, Barry Goldwater. The speech, today called "A Time for Choosing" was seen by many as a pivotal point in Reagan's political career.

The lessons he shared then are just as powerful and important today. In that speech, Reagan referred a story about freedom in which he said, "Not too long ago, two friends of mine were talking to a Cuban refugee, a businessman who had escaped from Castro, and in the midst of the story one of my friends turned to the other and said, 'We don't know how lucky we are.' And the Cuban stopped and said, 'How lucky you are? I had someplace to escape to.' And in that sentence, he told us the entire story. If we lose freedom here, there's no place to escape to. This is the last stand on earth."

Reagan went on to say that "we'll preserve for our children, this, the last best hope of man on earth, or we'll sentence them to take the last step into a thousand years of darkness."

In a way, those who have earned the Presidential Service Badge and those who support them are on the front lines of that preservation effort. They recognize that our Republic, for all its flaws, is still the last best hope of man on earth. That humility, born of service, exemplifies the best of America. Even today, despite our many challenges, externally and internally, these PSB recipients who were profiled and all others who wear the seal, help to make sure that the United States is still that "shining city on a hill."

FROM THE AUTHOR

A book like this isn't possible without the contributions of so many people before, during and after the writing process. For me, Washington DC, and particularly the White House, is a special place. It's more than just the heart of our government. It's a place where we can feel how the past impacts the present, in both subtle and in extraordinary ways.

Even an event like the annual White House Easter Egg Roll is a chance for us to create memories that tie us to the historical accounts

THE NO-FAIL MISSION

of the past. From my youngest daughter taking part in a traditional "Easter Egg Roll," it's not hard to extrapolate the feelings of a parent watching the same event take place, 30, 50, even 70 years prior.

To me, that's what makes the White House such a touchstone for Americans. It goes far beyond the party affiliation of the person who occupies the Oval Office. It goes far beyond the transitory nature of the people who work at the White House and at the entire Eighteen Acres complex. And it goes far beyond the fears, and even hopes, of the future that people feel when they walk inside those gates for the first time.

I was humbled to introduce some of those folks to you. As you have found, they are, to a man and to a woman, reflective about the missions they were asked to achieve on "behalf of a grateful nation." To them, you have my undying thanks for taking time out of your busy schedules to share your stories with me, and in turn, allowing me to share those stories with all of you.

I also want to thank my long-time George Washington University colleague and dear friend, Doctor Miguel Rodriguez. When Dr. Rodriguez, a Presidential Service Badge recipient himself, came to me with this proposal, I was uncertain if I would be willing to have the time to execute it, and to execute it at a level that these people deserved. At each step of this process, his belief in me never wavered. I never would have made it without you, sir.

I also want to thank my family for their steadfast support. As this book was being written, my three children were each dealing with significant changes in their lives. My oldest daughter, Elizabeth, had just been married and was settling into her new life several states away. My only son, Alex, was preparing for a move across the country to pursue a pair of PhDs in Psychology. My youngest daughter, Abigail, was getting ready for her senior year at university even as she was spending the summer helping others. My wife, Camille, was able to balance her summer between preparing for the upcoming school year, but to also be there, in person, to help our son make his successful move several hundred miles away.

They say each book changes its writer. That is certainly true in this case. For someone who teaches such things as American Government, Strategic Communications and Ethics on an undergraduate and graduate level, this book reaffirmed to me that these are not just abstract concepts to be taught in the sterile classroom. They are issues and ideas that mean little if there aren't strong men and women of character backing them up. I came away from each interview, concerned about the present, of course, but also confident about the future. For if each crisis provides us with people like these, who are willing to meet the moment with humility and grace, we truly have nothing to worry about.

Finally, I want to thank you, the reader. I am grateful each time a book like this gets your attention. It's not about me, it's about raising understanding and appreciation for those who have toiled away, out of the spotlight, not for their own personal glory, but for the glory of a nation. The same is true here.

So, thank you to one and all for being a part of such a remarkable project.

The Presidential Service Badge Foundation is dedicated to preserving the stories of valor and sacrifice of Presidential Service Badge awardees.

The author's proceeds from this book go to the Foundation's scholarship fund, which is designed to uplift family members through the awarding of academic scholarships to the institutions of their choice.

To learn more about these efforts, visit presidentialservicebadgefoundation.org

To send your tax-deductible donation to the scholarship fund, mail to:

The Presidential Service Badge Foundation
Scholarship Fund
PO Box 1062
Sylvania, OH 43560

Milton Keynes UK
Ingram Content Group UK Ltd.
UKHW022206130724
445341UK00008BA/175/J